LIFE

A User's Guide

ISBN: 978-0-615-39055-0
Copyright 2009, 2010 Cameron Smietana

"But it takes an awful long time to not write a book."
— **Douglas Adams**

To Kierce, Aspen, and Tierny

Chapters

1. God
2. Truth & God
3. Knowledge
4. Current Society
5. The Devil
6. The Fall
7. Perception
8. Love
9. Emotion
10. Evil
11. Hungry Ghost
12. Youth
13. War
14. One World
15. Time
16. Delusion
17. Ego
18. Communication
19. Initiating Action
20. Power
21. Coincidence
22. Morality
23. Trust
24. Self Doubt
25. To Fight
26. Freethinking
27. Mindfulness
28. Thought
29. Experience
30. Money
31. Drugs
32. Sex, Sin, & Self
33. Guilt
34. Happiness
35. Leadership
36. Discipline
37. Crime
38. Personal Responsibility
39. Girls & Boys
40. Body & Mind
41. Death
42. Quality of Life

1.

God

God does not forsake anyone. Ever. We who say we have been forsaken by God have rather forsaken God ourselves. We should clear something up right away here before we go any further. God is not sitting in a chair, in some gathering of clouds in the sky surrounded by angels and golden shiny things and dead relatives. God is not a male or a female. Neither is God both. Is there a gender to a star? Does a solar system have sex with another solar system? Does an atom of hydrogen try to sweet talk and buy gifts for an atom of helium because it's got some atomic jungle fever? Does a cloud seeing a nearby cloud with great curves try to buy it some drinks and bring it home after the sun sets?

Now some people are going to get all crazy here and say something to the effect of, "Well you see, at some points an atom will attract another atom with a variance in it's electron shells and they will exchange an electron or two in order to re-establish a balance and this is reminiscent of a male giving up his sperm to the female's egg."

It is called an interaction and that happens between most everything in existence regardless of if you are a man and a woman kissing or a man and another man exchanging sports stats. How many times today have you had an interaction with a toilet? Would you consider making an exchange from your bowels to the bottom of the bowl an act of sex?

Now let's get back to this issue of God being somehow a person that has a long beard and looks exceedingly wise and gentle and likes to wear robes. There is a process by which religions and cultures pull their own belief systems from an array of those surrounding and predating them. In order not to drag this out let's just jump back a bit to the Greeks and Romans. Most of you should have a rudimentary knowledge of the history of the Greeks and Romans and if not perhaps you should turn off the TV or watch more of the history and discovery channels than the food network and Fox. In early western history the gods were depicted as wearing togas, were the bearers of all knowledge to mankind, and some in particular had just the loveliest of white beards. Now you can go and call this coincidental, you can also hit yourself in the face with a frying pan, but I wouldn't recommend it. Check out some art history.

  There is an undeniable chain of cause and effect evident within the level of existence where humans and our actions tend to reside, and henceforth we can trace the Lotus Esprit to the Model T Ford and observe the evolution of the automobile. Through paintings and sculptures especially, you can trace the modern western image of God back through the ages, even prior to the Greeks should you want, and witness for yourself the pulling of customs in reference to God and the gods cross-culturally throughout our history.

  Continuing on, consider those that believe that their religious text is The Word of God. Idiots. And here's why: as is quite evident in art, the common source of our western God's imagery isn't even of one religion but that of many. Things such as dietary laws, angels, spirits, monotheism, virgin births via angels or God, etc... All can be found in cultures and religions long dead that have predated the births of our modern religions.

  If this isn't convincing enough let's take one text in particular into consideration, The Bible. As is quite well documented, this Christian text was put together under a summit held by the Emperor Constantine. At this conference, Christian leaders from all over the Roman empire were brought together to decide once and for all on a common religious text to unite, not only the bickering Christians, but also the empire of which they were citizens. During this time together these church heads decided whether or not to put in the different chapters of the book. These men coming from all the lands of the empire had vastly different ideas as to what should stay and what should go. They came from lands still steeped in pagan customs, and favored books that reflected their regions' cultural beliefs. Some wanted stories of big fish that people lived inside of. Some wanted stories of water converting into wine as well as walking on water. Others wanted the simple story of a man that grew up a poor carpenter and through his own trials and tribulations found God and helped others to become better people and closer to God. Well, we all know the end result. But do not only consider that these men were not uncorrupted by their cultures and the intermingling of multiple sets of beliefs, but also that this collections of books was sponsored by the emperor of Rome for political reasons.

 Were it that an uneducated and illiterate person suddenly woke one morning and very publicly ran to a very public place and very publicly started writing words of which he did not know and wrote an entire religious text in such a manner until he was finished and then, still needing someone to read it back to him, was shocked by what it said, then it would perhaps suffice that something extraordinary involving the hand of God had happened here, and that this text MAY be the Word of God.

Some will say that we must have faith including in a book of God, regardless of religion. Faith is not faith if it is blind. Just as being a blind patriot and calling ourselves to arms at the wave of a flag without understanding what it is we are rattling the saber at is not true patriotism. One must have faith, yes. One must also have logic, sound judgment and seek the truth, and this truth can be found in all things including lies. There is a difference that must be recognized between truth and fact if you are to fully understand faith. Those that are Word of God-ers take religious text as fact and fact as truth and in that have faith. This is at best an ill-conceived notion, and at worst not even a conceived notion, but is something in which a person is not even conscious of but solely assumes out of sloth. Truth is not found simply by reading a word, it takes contemplation and determination. Truth is experienced; unlike fact, it is not a concept which can be comprehended in a black and white fashion.

Books of God have always been written literally by the hand of man though they may figuratively be written by the hand of God. Anything ever written by man is corrupted by him. This is not to say that there is not truth within, but that the times in which a man lives, the customs of his culture, the political and economic environment, etc, all play a part in how this writer will translate his spiritual knowledge to ink and paper. To have faith in anything less is simply ignorant and lazy minded.

2.

Truth & God

Truth is inexplicable. The true nature of things is hidden from us by our very nature, by the nature of this plane of existence, that is to say the nature of duality. Our existence is ruled by opposing forces: Hot and cold, good and evil, right and wrong, matter and energy. Often times spiritual masters will give their students a phrase or saying to think upon, sometimes a question for the student to conceive an answer to. Then when the students come back thinking they have the answer, or have contemplated long enough, the teacher will hand them a new phrase to contemplate in diametric opposition to the first. The master, if he does give an answer, will give one that is the exact opposite of what would make logical sense. This is done to illustrate to the student the paradoxical nature of existence and the futility of trying to escape it. Until we understand the paradox of reality as what it truly is, and understand what it means to all things in the all the worlds, we know absolutely nothing. Then again, when we reach that point, we know nothing again.

Words can be used all day and all night for a thousand years but until duality is understood through direct experience the illusion that is reality cannot be understood. An ancient once said to the effect, "If there was ever a man that had never known words I would like to speak with him." Clearly a man that has never known words has still had a life full of experience, but how does he convey these conceptualized ideas without words? Likewise it is quite recognized that words are meaningless without the common experiences we associate with them. What is heaven? This is an abstract concept of which few, if any, can credibly speak. We use it as a tool when opposed to hell as a means to quell the more barbarous and ignorant of us into subservience for the social good. But if this place really does exist how can it even begin to be described without firsthand experience?

When we talk we use common terminology to convey ideas, desires and objectives, to tell stories and make requests. But when telling a story does the speaker convey his direct experience to the listener or does the listener compare all these words to his own past experiences? As such it is impossible for a person that has experienced the Holy Spirit or momentary nirvana to convey to the unbeliever, uninitiated or inexperienced, that which is beyond the paradoxical duality of our day to day world.

Now don't think for a second that God, or what have you, is something only to be found somewhere beyond our daily world. It is very much the opposite. It is with the proper mindset that one is to be in with communion with God, not something of which you can only do in deep meditation, sleep or after death. When Ram Das says "Be Here Now!" or when Alan Watts refers to the ever present moment, they are speaking of experiencing this communion of mind, body, and soul, right here and right now.

This God or infinite spirit is all pervasive. Some would say that thinking such would mean one is a believer in pantheism or earth worship, and although these are not bad in themselves, this is not quite a correct view. This problem arrives from the mindset of dualism where all things are opposed by something and our popular scientific mind, which categorizes all things into cute consumable bundles. This God, this thing, is above all description and encompasses all things.

Neither is it good or bad. Nor is it both or neither. What then is this thing we call God? As is readily apparent there is no explanation for it, it is something only to be experienced. Should we search it, we will find it.

People ask "how can God be in all things"? How is He in a dingo and a murderer and a lifeless asteroid all at once? For believers in God I will ask this: Where was everything before your God created it? Before anything existed where was God? If God was there before existence and He was the only thing then what did He create this existence out of? There is nothing that can come from nothing nor can anything be turned to nothing, so wouldn't it be logical to presume that everything that came to light from God was of God? As in the tale of Eve being created of Adam's rib, the whole of existence was created of a part of God. As for the non-believers I would ask this: What do you know about quantum mechanics, string theory, hyper-dimensional physics, dynamics, chaos theory, etc..? If all of these theories (and more) are combined into a philosophical viewpoint (which I know you have a hard time with) what do you observe? A system in which nothing is separate and all is inter-related, non-local communication over vast distances is commonplace; all things that make up our universe (matter/energy) are only defined by their apparent opposition to each in Newtonian science, while they are clearly the same "stuff" in advanced sciences. What do you call a system that crosses many dimensions, contains all things within (which are in constant communication) and is apparently made of nothing but itself?

We all hear of God being omnipotent and omnipresent. And most of us feel it somewhere deep inside before ever hearing it from another. We know of the laws of nature which default to efficiency as the status quo. Would it not be most efficient to create all things of yourself and be ever present in them than to create out of nothing, most assuredly hard to do, and then observe all things at once through an innumerable amount of godly telescopes and televisions and other instruments receiving signals from sensors all over existence that are somehow invisible and not really part of that existence? And then how does God observe the things that God is observing with? This would be a most ineffective means of being the Godhead!

It may seem that we have stumbled away from the vague subject of truth, but the subject of truth cannot truly be spoken of without the delving into God, the source, the ground of all being, the only truth. The only thing. One!

In short, know that truth is found through wisdom and wisdom is begotten from logical study, and direct experience of material and immaterial existence. Truth is far from fact. Fact describes objects 100% in the material and measurable world, whereas truth crosses planes and describes both the material and immaterial. It is just as important therefore that we understand our spirituality and consciousness, as well as material subject matter if we truly seek truth.

3.

Knowledge

Knowledge can be found in all places and in many ways. Nothing that you encounter in life is completely useless. Books, movies, random conversations at a cafe or in passing at a gas station, a scribbled note that floats by in the water or blows down the sidewalk past your feet. Many of us go through life like the three little monkeys, see no evil, hear no evil, speak no evil. When we develop actions and habits from the fears of the unknown, we become isolated from the world around us. Then we turn into those monkeys and stop truly learning. When life is lived in such a way the flavor of life is lost.

There are two ways to adapt to all the inundations of life. Firstly and most popularly, is to attach oneself to a strict and simplistic set of beliefs early on in life that explain away most of one's questions. In this we are like a stone and our mind atrophies to a state that is resistant to change, our learning is severely blocked. In such a state as this we are resistant against any new or contradictory ideas. With our conception of reality held in this manner, if we are to come across any information that contradicts our mindset to a staggering degree, our reality will become pulverized as stone does when assaulted by a larger force. And then we will be left to pick up the pieces.

The second adaptation and more rare than I feel is healthy for humanity is to be as water, constantly adapting and encompassing subjects we encounter. In such a state we do not dwell upon any one fact as truth but constantly flow from subject to subject learning and forming our own thoughts from many sources.

When something is encountered that is contradictory to something we have previously taken for true fact we do not block against it as stone but encompass it as we have previous ideas and pull it along the stream with us as we do our other ideas until we come to a conclusion. Then as we let this floating twig of an idea escape our immediate attentions we will carry along our new conclusion as a fluid concept ready to be adapted at a moments notice to any further contradictions. And thus there is never any resistance to the mind and knowledge is gathered unbiased from a multitude of sources. And here a degree of wisdom is attained from our experience of logical adaptations of the mind to the many paradoxes of life.

When studying different government or religions or philosophies, there is always a difference of opinions. The goal on our part in studying them should not be on deciding which is right or wrong and thus perpetuating the dualistic mindset that is our shackles, but to read between the lines and find in them the current of truth that is pervading throughout. In doing this we will find liberation and this course will lead us to discovering real knowledge, real wisdom and perhaps the infinite spirit.

4.

Current Society

If ever there was an oxymoronic arrangement of terms it would include civility and society. I have witnessed more civility in those that dwell on the edges of society than I have in those who consider themselves of high society. Those who live out on the periphery are most times more noble than those of noble birth. There is something here that has much to do with the balance of self sufficiency and dependency.

On the fringes of society we tend to find those that are in general self aware and hold a respect of living life. These people are not the downtrodden souls of the lower class who feel social binds to church and state and are cast as mindless drones to work in the factories and mega corporations. People of the periphery are where they are by choice. Most of them are highly intelligent and self educated if not college educated. Largely they have been involved in criminal acts, for they do not regard the law of man as the law of God, though I would dare not call them criminals as they are the soul of man; they are the embodiment of the forgotten freedoms of our ancestors.

These are not the blind patriots and blind faithful. These men and women, though they maybe lawless, may hold odd jobs seamlessly going from warehouse, to corporate office, to mountainside without much of a fuss. They are unattached to the material world and therefore do not attempt to grasp hold of material gains for the sheer sake of possession. Unlike the majority of humans in our modern society they are not seeking the fruitless gains of material wealth, but with their meager materials share bonds of true and open relationships fearlessly among a diversity of odd characters within their underground.

These are our painters, musicians, and poets. These are our artists. Many we will run into that have not produced art for perhaps years at a time, but such is the mind and the soul of the artist, as they are not bound by the social demands for bigger, better and faster production. In these people we will find the best of man often times wrapped within psychosis: sometimes vanity, sometimes depression, sometimes worse. But though they may lack in productive stability, they possess a fearlessness many of us lack. Some of these artists will convey their confusions into art, others into their triumphs. While others yet will find the source of their existence and, finding existence in vain, live life itself as art, following out their strangest whims.

To these people, society and its strict lines are only as real as any other imagination. They embrace society when it serves them and shun it when it does not. It is not something of which is used to judge themselves and their neighbors by, nor something by which to falsely imply security and cling to as a life preserver in a turbulent existence. They are not dependent upon the opinion of another to feel good about themselves though they would not condemn one that laid upon them praise. They do not look with envy at wealth and riches but they would not throw them away either to be poor, unless they knew that wealth would corrupt them spiritually.

They are peaceful and tender hearted. They are passionate while lovers and dispassionate while logicians. They would not conquer and enforce ideals on men but would rather have men educated on their differences and revel in their varieties. Their common fear is of the cage and uniformity. There is a phrase quoted in a book by Vonnegut that says, "while there is a soul in prison, I am not free," and to me this calls to mind the spirit of freedom and the soul of the scoundrel, the artist, the smuggler. These are the most genuine specimens of humanity you will encounter. They are the best of us and the worst of us. If the mainstream ideals of our society were the ideals held by this group, we may not all live in mansions and have fancy imported cars, but life would be much better off.

Having touched on the fringe of society, hardly to be considered a class thereof, let's speak of the working classes. We have here two subclasses, the lower class and the middle class. Now some are going to want to divide these further into lower class, lower middle, upper middle, and lower upper classes but in truth it is not the upper class which works, they may have jobs and careers but do not in effect work for subsistence but for pride and power. And for the time being, we will concern ourselves with those who work from fear of starvation, homelessness, social pressures, and family dependency.

In the lower class we find a dependency on the system and entrapment brought about by two key factors: one being lack of intelligence or poor education, the other being attachment to familial dependents. Of the first instance we can observe that a person through poor education or lack of intelligent faculties is perpetually relegated to the service of the middle and upper classes through his lack of understanding the basic premises of our institutions. The secondary instance aforementioned describes one whom, though intelligent, fell into marriage or bore children at a time before they understood the structures of society and will henceforth be working perhaps two low wage jobs part or full time for most of their adult life in order to support their dependents.

The lower class will be the assistant to the machine operator or the janitor, fast food cook or superstore checkout attendant. They will make just enough money to pay their bills if they are lucky, and be forever cast into debt when they are one day forced to rack up charges on a credit card or get a payday loan to pay their rent or feed their family. Lack of prosperity as such makes it quite easy to take funds from government in the way of welfare and forms a great dependency on a massive scale.

Eventually over generations of welfare, this social program eats away at the beliefs in the lower class of self reliance and freedom, hence making government their master. They are ignorant or actively dismissive that the government that is paying them a fee for sustenance is occupied and controlled by those very people in whose factories and mega-stores they sweat away their lives, where their souls are withered away for a pitiful wage. I am reminded of Jim Morrison singing, "Trade in your hours for a handful of dimes". The lower class is indeed a modern slave class, now referred to as wage slaves.

In the middle class we find a whole different animal. Though this class also is attached to family for much of it's aspirations it is not attached to it by despair as the lower class. Here we find the office worker and the factory managers, the unionized construction worker and other skilled workers and urban professionals. This class is mostly motivated by pride of family and envy of the upper class. These people strive to put their children in the fanciest new style of clothes and the newest sports gear, while putting themselves in the newest shiniest automobile as well as stationing their family in the most prestigious bland suburb nearest them in the most expensive cookie cutter house.

Trapped as well in a cycle of toil and debt, their toil more mental and debt more apparent on paper than in the refrigerator, they tend not to move higher in class but do not fall to far below. The unspoken bond between society and the middle class is that so long as they do not seek power to affect change of the status quo and hence ruin the profits, power and designs of the upper class, the middle class will be well fed, housed, clothed, and entertained. This good behavior will earn them relative freedom of movement throughout the realm of that society.

In the middle class we find the blind patriot and those of blind faith for it is this class that specializes in self-deception for the sake of self-preservation. The desire here is not solely to survive as in the lower class but to survive in a comfortable and over-protective manner. No bad food, no bad people, no bad places, no bad thoughts. Here more than the lowest and the highest classes, the people fear outsiders, for here uniformity is personified and diversity is persecuted. Day in and day out, for years and decades, there is no change, no drama, no joy of life. Masquerading as freedom through materialism, it is a desert nearly devoid of true human spirit.

Most of us will never meet the true upper class, these captains of industry and rulers of countries and continents. They have something in common with our artists in that they understand the facade that is society. To them it is but a toy and they play with it amongst themselves as they would as if it were only a game of chess. The lower class is simply a pawn to them or less, the middle class their knights and bishops. But the upper classes are not to be mistaken for the kings and queens of the board for if they would lose to their opponent they would not fall but rather play another round. Do not mistake, they are the players, and hence our controllers.

The fanaticism bred socially into the consciousness of the middle and lower classes is but a tool to these chess masters. When a modern international corporatist plays nation against nation it is not for want of a set of ideals to prevail in the hearts and minds of the nation to be conquered, but to further their own interests in power and control.

The main differentiation between the artist's view of life as game and that of the ruling elite is that for the artist, all men have intrinsic value and it is distasteful to subjugate them in any fashion, whereas for our unelected masters, so long as they themselves, their family and peers are not subjugated it is not at all distasteful for other men to have no value.

The true upper class is not subject to laws for they write them. They are not in fear of religions for they finance them. They are not afraid of populations and countries for they own them. Ever wonder what Intelligence Agencies and Black-Ops are for? "National Defense" is just another way of saying "Investment Protection".

5.

The Devil

Literal interpretations frustrate me. On the subjects of religion, God, and the devil, we are always finding these literal takings. Laziness of mind and fear of the unknown bring about such things and if we can't quite conquer ourselves, little of anything anyone writes will be of any use to anybody else. Nor will any of us be of much use to mankind as we perpetuate ill cycles.

As is tiresome to say but must be said, our common image of devil can be traced back through history in western cultures. The first thought that comes to my mind as a singular entity similar to the devil is Hades. Hades wasn't necessarily a bad God, he just happened to have a job in which he controlled the realm of the afterlife. It wasn't even hell as we perceive it now. Even before the Greeks there was an underworld and a land of the dead. Now enter the Catholic Church.

Of course as we have seen, cultures do not die, they simply fade into others. The land of the dead of the Greeks and Romans was divided into the Christian kingdom of the Father, heaven, and the hell for which all pagans and unbelievers would suffer in all eternity if they did not convert. And we think psychological warfare to be a new technique. Not only were Christians united under a common book for the sake of control, but their old Gods, if they could not be completely replaced in the guise of saints and angels, were converted into demons and the devil. Hence, former gods such as Neptune, Baal and Pan etc, were combined into the figure of the devil. Observe the horns of Baal, the hoofed legs of Pan and the triton of Neptune.

Now with this figure or slight variances thereof throughout the western world, we have ourselves a tool for the brainwashing of youths. Terrifying images of this devil and his demons were made in paintings and sculptures commissioned by the church. Christianity as the state religion of the Roman Empire spread through the cities of Europe. Here the burghers, city dwellers like our modern suburbanites, had little use for religion other than as an organizing establishment, praying only when they are in crisis, their children are sick or when at church on Sunday as to be seen by others for the sake of pride.

It is a little harder to spread a faith to people of the land such as farmers and huntsmen who are attached to ancient customs and deities. Well, suffice it to say that after a few generations of taking wares to town for trade and conversing and intermarrying and doing such things as humans will do, the psychological tools of the church succeeded in turning the Gods of our ancestral fathers into our current demons and devils.

Now that we have touched on the modern western conception of the devil as a literal being, we may proceed into why such a conception is utter rubbish and what this devil is in actuality. The usage of a conception of the devil as a literal being is of no spiritual necessity and serves only to use the basest of our own fears against us in order to make us subservient to a social structure. Our base fears are of pain and confinement. To be brainwashed from a young age that if you don't fall into lock step with the social order you will be condemned to eternity in a place where you suffer endless torment at the hands of a frightful beast is quite an effective means of control.

I presume that you are familiar with the concept of fables. These stories are told in such manner as to present a moral or lesson which can then be applied to everyday life. Think in this manner of religious texts as you read between the lines and you will find the following when concerning the Devil.

The Devil is the attachment to the material world in denial of the spiritual. He is the supreme trickster that convinces us that we are separated from God and not of Him. He tells us that we are here by accident of science and that science is separate from God. He tells us we can fill that hole inside of us, which many of us do not realize is there, with drugs and sex and fine possessions. The Devil tells us God is dead. He tells to not dwell on God but to dwell instead upon ourselves and to become selfish.

Now don't be a tool and say, "Hey, you just said the Devil isn't a person and now you're saying he is telling me this stuff!". You see, the Devil is not a being but a spirit or common thought that passes through the consciousness of mankind. He is temptation, denial, deception, wrath, condescension etc... In short, he is the seven sins of Christendom that when embraced, deny the eightfold path of the Buddha. From these seven sins, stem all human evils. It is the initial denial of ourselves being of God that the hole within us is formed and it is the Devil that tempts us to fill it by means other than communion.

I am reminded of a story told by the Lama Surya Das: A poor man, having a dream that in another city under a bridge there lay a treasure, decides to travel there. While he scopes out the bridge a soldier notices him standing there and approaches him and asks of him what he is standing around for? The poor man tells him and the soldier laughs saying he had a similar dream that in another town under a house laid a treasure. The poor man inquired as to this house and town and finding that it was his, returned home. When he returned home he found the treasure buried beneath his own hearth. This story illustrates that not only should we appreciate what we have in our own lives, but also that in the home that is our body, our mind, our soul, we can find what it is that we are looking for and find that we are after all not poor / spiritually empty.

As a quick note I would like add here that I wouldn't recommend giving up all worldly things unless you are quite content to stop eating and breathing and go to your death. Pleasures of this world are to be enjoyed as the pains are to be suffered equally. The problem with pleasures arises when we attempt to stop feeling pain so that we may only feel pleasure whether it be through constant eating of rich food or of delighting in sex or alcohol. When this happens we quickly lose the flavor of life and the ability to enjoy those things that we so did enjoy. Here we find ourselves taking in more and more drugs to feel good again or making bad deals for more money or doing terrible acts to advance our careers and so on. This is addiction. It is not a disease to be treated by abstinence but through balance, personal contemplation and direct confrontation of our demons. We must embrace our devil within that he may hold us no more. When considering physical pleasure whether of possessions or of actions we must take all things in moderation including moderation. We must also remember not to attach to ourselves a dependency upon "things". This life is ephemeral and what may be today sure and steady, tomorrow is gone.

6.

The Fall

Two tales come to my mind. One of the Devil being cast out of heaven, the other of man being cast out of the garden. These are very much related in my mind. Let's first speak of the tale of the Garden of Eden.

In Eden we have here two people who live in bliss and when they gain the ability of knowledge, they lose said bliss. This can be considered to be when man first became self aware, developing consciousness of self. No longer was he one with the macro-organism of the earth, living contentedly alongside other creatures in perfect weather in land that is plentiful with food, or equally contentedly in the arid land in terrible weather without regarding himself as a foe of the earth.

Life stopped being full of timeless moments that simply were what they were, and things became good and bad. Man, realizing that he could build shelters to stand the worst of storms and could stock up on foods for winter, stopped his natural migrations as scavengers and became hunters and then farmers attached to their lands. The freedom our animalistic ancestor had known was gone, replaced by the ever present anxieties of control, structure, production, time etc... By giving up the ignorance of knowledge man had decided not to follow the natural order of things. A new order was established in the form of society, and being contradictory to our animalistic nature, to this day is still found quite uncomfortable to many of its residents as we are constantly plagued by anxiety, depression, suicide, murder, the list goes on.

Still though, it is possible to have freedom of mind and soul regardless of our society and knowledge. The means to this is in remaining unattached to those things that we are not already attached to and dis-attaching one's self from those things of which we currently are attached. This is done through the acknowledgment that nothing in this existence is static and that all is transitory. We are always complaining that being dis-attached sounds cold and heartless, but consider the following for it is not so.

    We speak of being dis-attached, not being distant of heart. To be not attached is to follow the course of nature which clings to nothing. Continents that we have lived upon for countless ages were once submerged or lifeless. The tallest mountains were once just flat ground that has over time been pushed up by earthquakes and the force of colliding tectonic plates. Planets, solar systems, the universe have all been in different forms at different times. It is only through our self-denial, our denial of nature, that we consider things to be of permanence. Property, relationships, wealth, status, all things in life with which we interact are in constant flux and our constant fight to stabilize and unify and to hold onto a perfect ideal is not only fruitless but is unhealthy for the mind and the spirit. Is it not better to let go and accept fate as it affects us? This is by no means saying that if we are a doctor we should not go on with our work, or that if we are in love that we should not try to make our lover happy and content. No, this is saying that when we are following through the actions we take in life we must not allow ourselves to be upset by their outcomes, as we do not/cannot/never will control life.

    There is no need of a constant fear of the future and of what may be, nor is there need to dwell on the past and what might have been. Things are as they are, and there is absolutely nothing we can do about it! We must use our past mistakes to improve ourselves in the future and ensure that we do not worry that in the future we should make mistakes. We cannot delude ourselves into thinking that we are in control of our lives. We must be in the ever present moment and do our best and be our best now.

You see, there is very little room in this world for free will and hence for blaming ourselves. Since the beginning of time countless variables have been in action driving us to the current moment. For example I may have just decided to smoke a cigarette. How can I really say that this was my decision? How many variables have propelled me to my current situation? My parents and upbringing, culture, social pressures, personal tastes developed from social standards and physical tendencies, my mental state as affected by all of the above and more... it is impossible to lay out here all of the variables from the very start of things till now that have set me up to possibly smoke that cigarette. Very well you may say "You have been pushed to this point by various circumstances but in the end whilst you pull the cigarette from the pack it is your choice as to smoke it or not, it is free will." Is it? Convince me.

That gut response in which we make split second decisions is also programming. From birth we establish tendencies in our actions and habits. These habits, though not rules, decide for us in most case our actions. In the case of stopping fully at a stop sign or getting up early to work out we tend to default to our habits as a form of automation. Although it may be possible to observe our personal habits and thereby change them so that we may choose differently the next time we think of smoking a cigarette, why did we observe our habits in the first place? What drove that action and in turn what initiated that and so on. Regardless of what we do or how we change, all was set in motion from the beginning and though we are accountable for our actions for we are their instrument, we are not guilty of what we do for we haven't the slightest control. Only the illusion of control exists.

We finally reach the other story! So we have the children's tale of God making an angel and this angel rebelling, deciding he can do a better job than God. There is a tussle and God surprisingly turns out to still be God and casts the rebelling angel out of heaven and this angel then decides to spite God and do everything he can against him. This angel becomes the Devil. This represents the beginning of creation. We have already spoken of the division of existence into dualities and opposing forces and this will come into play again here.

Imagine, if you will, the ground of all being. Imagine everything, every time, everywhere all combined in one point. Also in this source we find every opposite of these as well as every possibility in between. Here is infinite possibility. Here lies absolute nothingness. Here is the inconceivable and unknowable God. Now imagine a God that dreams a million dreams. All possibilities are known to him, all nothingness as well. In some dreams there are worlds and space and time. In other dreams there are realms of which we cannot begin to imagine. Some dreams are only emptiness.

Now imagine a dream that begins in void. Then suddenly the void is split into halves of opposition, light and dark, matter/energy, time and space. All of these splits continue happening as one stick being cut into five or all the shades of gray being formed from black and white. This continues on for countless ages until an apex is reached from which all possible creations of this splitting has commenced. Then after the summit has been reached another epoch commences where these forms recombine and slowly head back to the everything-void from whence they sprang.

But this dream never ends, it only starts again anew as it is one of countless possibilities that lie within God that can never not be; as a record that is played over and over, though it is never played. This whole creation of reality by duality is illusion. For in truth there is no duality in God. There is only God. There is only one time, one moment. The time of no time.

Consider the Devil as follows: He is the trickster that convinces us that not only do we exist separate of God, but that we actually exist! He is the dream itself, the element of God who has decided to play hide and seek with Himself. For as you are now perhaps sitting and reading in your home, it is in truth God reading words written on God sitting comfortably on God in a shelter built of God.

7.
Perception

Everything we hold dear is pure perception as is everything we hate. We would like to think that existence is not only quite easily defined, but universally perceived. We presume that because two people may be pointing at an object and call it, let's say a brick, it therefore is perceived as the same thing by both parties. This is a wild assumption. But how, if I observe that the brick is red and rough and of certain measurements and my friend agrees. can we be both seeing something different?

What if the color I see when you say red I see as blue? What if the texture I feel when you say rough is to me smooth or soft? Perhaps even what you call a brick with square edges I see as a totally different shape.

From the earliest age we are taught that names ARE what things are. But a name is not what something is; a name is a common agreement as to what to refer to something as. By all means what I see as I walk through a forest you may see as towering leprechauns for trees, large tufts of cotton candy for bushes and unicorns for deer. The scent of the pines may even smell like pina colada. I have absolutely no way of knowing and neither do you.

Assumptions upon perceptions bring about expectations. When we perceive that a tendency exists for a particular outcome, we assume from our observations that we may expect a similar outcome in the future. But why is attachment made to our expectations? This rises from a need within us to feel in control, as well as an attachment stemming from our lack of living in the here and now.

It's a funny thing, the subject of desires and being here now. To be in the now we have to be unattached from desire. To be free of desire we have to be in the now. In actuality those are elements of a multi-pronged attack that takes us to a more grounded state. Part of attaining enlightenment, liberation, heaven or whatever we would like to call it begins with cultivating these two concepts into cooperating functions, operating within our everyday lives.

Let's imagine that you are at work and having a horrible time because you cannot wait to get home to your significant other. The hours drag on and on and life seems to be all the more miserable. Simply put, you need to quell your desire to be with your loved one in the future and instead focus your consciousness in the moment in which you are actually living. This is what is referenced in the saying "letting go" or "whatever will be will be". We have to accept fate for what it is and realize that though we may have an iota of symbolic control in our lives, in all actuality we have none, and that to worry, though it makes us feel more human, is exceedingly useless. All forms of worry into future things are an evil that sucks away our life. The illusion of future is a demon that, pulling our consciousness away from the ever-present moment, (the only one moment that ever truly exists) is in effect feeding off our sin every time we allow ourselves to be deceived.

As we talked earlier about habits and addictions filling holes within us, worry is also a form of addiction. Every time that we worry about the future this habit becomes that much more ingrained in our psyche. Over time we cannot help but cast our consciousness out of the moment.

Beyond this, when we observe that when we worry over things out of our control and they sometimes work out, we then feel equally inclined to worry more the next time. If we worry about something so much and then it turns out good we feel obligated out of superstition to worry the same amount the next time. If the outcome is bad we feel that we ought to redouble our efforts the next time and perhaps the outcome will be good. This is clearly an absurd addiction!

When we allow base emotions and unfounded assumptions to suppress the young buddings within our minds, our perceptions of the world become expectations and desires. These expectations then fuel the guards residing in our heads that hold the chains of our own captivity. When desires and fear-driven control are overcome by the power of our will, our awareness of Self will begin to flower.

Though we will never be able to perceive the world of any other person it is imperative that we do not consider our own world view as the only and best possible world view.

8.

Love

A strange and wonderful thing love is. Art, science, philosophy, religion, all things in humanity pay tribute to love. To some the word itself raises feelings ranging from fear to bliss. This writing itself would remain incomplete were it not to mention love. There are many kinds of love which any idiot can observe but here first we will converse about the love of family.

Most of us have been raised with parents or siblings, and those of us that have not are very likely to become married or have children of our own. There is a bond by blood that is undeniable. Something ineffable. Although the love of family is of importance to social stability and the shaping of individuals it is important to note that we should not be completely influenced by the affections of familial relations.

As in any social structure those with opinions differing from the masses and those holding the reigns of power are persecuted and outcast. If we are to depend too fully on the love of our family and they should fail to attend to our expectations, our image of self and that of our family may be shattered. If there is ever a conflict of interest, we are likely to question both the sanctity of the family and the identity of ourselves. Again, it is not advised to be distant from our families and build ourselves an impenetrable wall in which nothing can affect us, but in this arena as well, we should be as flowing water and fully encompass all possible confrontations. In this state we will be generous in giving and receiving love, and not become discontented from its withholding.

It is important that should we be in the power of a family not to suppress those who hold a different viewpoint than our own and deny them affections but to bring to public forum their disagreement and disarm their follies with logic as well admit to when our own reason has faltered. To deny affections or to rule with a disrespecting iron fist will accomplish in the end the instability of our families through rebellious attitudes and actions, as well as affecting the mindset of those under our charge to feel unloved, disrespected, and possibly isolated and possibly not worthy of being loved. If the foundations of respect and love of the castle that is our family is destroyed, the facade may stand but the main structure will fail. I find nothing useful with facades other than for those who, discontent with themselves and their lives, wish to court the approval of others so that they may fulfill their pathetic desire to be accepted into a mindless mob of sinful judges.

The love of family is generally stable and has about it a relaxed nature. Our next type of love to be examined is much more lively. This love of which we speak is the love of passion. Love that, like a wave, whisks away worry and care and then comes crashing back with a vengeance, full of despair. I have witnessed many people that run off cliffs at the chance of embracing passionate love and just as many that run from it. To run from love is to be afraid. This fear stems from various sources which include among them fear of happiness, of pain and of chance.

To be afraid of happiness occurs when we are convinced that we are undeserving of love and that for some reason or other we deserve to suffer. This is a very unhealthy attitude and only serves to perpetuate a sense of loneliness and unwelcoming of love. What may be the cause? We may feel that we are undeserving because we have done a horrible deed that we are a bad person, etc. It is solely up to us to rectify ourselves with our previous actions and assuage ourselves of any guilt or negative feelings.

Behind door number two we have the fear of pain. To fear pain is a natural evolution of mind and is by no account shameful. Fearing pain can be extremely silly and cause unneeded self-inflicted grief when imposed upon love. This fear thrives when we have our mind focused on the past and the future rather than in the here and now. We worry about what negatives have happened involving love in the past and comically attempt to apply predictions to the future. "I have been hurt in the past therefore I shall not involve myself with love and be saved in the future!" Stupendously ridiculous. This line of thinking is unhealthy in that it will not only isolate us from others, but also in that it is a black and white mindset. These black and white outlooks are like viruses that spread to other aspects of our mindsets and can have devastating effects.

Here again I find myself being exhaustively redundant. This mindset of denying love for fear of pain is as if we are trying to be a solid mass that is resistant to change. If we perhaps took an opinion that love would last forever and play perfectly into our wishes and love, clearly not being a thing to be contained within walls, destroyed the walls in which we conceived it, we are sure to be disappointed to say the least. If then we attempt to build stronger and thicker walls we have learned the wrong lesson. We may have presumed that it was the forces of love which were wrong and not our mindset when in truth it was our mindset being built in stone that was to be avoided. At the moment our walls fall, we have the option to become fluid as water or rebuild our bullheaded mental constructs. If we continue to suffer as a result of our own poor choices, how can we continue to blame anything but ourselves?

Finally, the fear of chance. This problem relates to the above in that it is also focused in obsessions with past and future. But fear of chance appears to be more related to a material mindset than to our preferring a womb of denial. Like a banker we sometimes calculate decision by risk. "Is love worth my time?" "Will I have time for my work if I am out looking for love?" "Will my affectionate actions towards my lover take away from those things I wish to do for myself?" Rather than delving into the moment and tasting the fruits of our labors we can find ourselves continually looking for the next best thing, the next possession. For those of us that act in this manner it matters very little if we have a mass of wealth, we are always either melancholy or maintain a facade of joviality which is consistently distant. When we are stuck in this state not much can help us, for we would rather sacrifice our soul for material gain than to risk the chance that a love affair may interrupt our schemes for power and control. We may have lovers but we will not enjoy true loving. When we are self centered and have no love to give anyone but ourselves, no one will trade their love for our negligence. We may chance upon a person that will follow us around as a dog, lavishing us with their affections but we will still be unable to enjoy them for we will still be closed of heart and likely we will even look down upon them for loving as so freely while we love them not at all, further distancing us from them.

All this time and still we have not addressed those cliff divers of love, the romantics. "It is better to have loved and lost," they say. I would be hard pressed to disagree with them. Romantics do not fear that they will be hurt, for they know they may be but press on without regard or regret. It is honorable and brave to follow love in such a manner, but I would like to make the reader wary of an addiction thus formed. With this lack of regard for personal suffering at times can come a lack of personal understanding, in that we may be reluctant to observe any follies on our part within our relationships and will blame any failures upon others. By never fearing to run to love and sacrificing much of our material life of money, time, and attention we may feel that we do enough to make love last. Sometimes when we are in the role of cliff jumpers we are so enthralled with the passions of a new love that we never observe our own mistakes when it comes time for the natural excitement of a new relationship to die down. At this point rather than adapting to the new requirements of ourselves to continue on in this love affair, we become distraught at the parting of the passion that until then had defined the relationship. Subtleties that escape us can soon cause the affair to be a memory. Although jumping in for love may be admirable, if we do not maintain our adaptive abilities and remain subject to change, we may very well end up on a cyclical hunt. Always searching for a high, then the losing it, then again we find it and so on.

  This love business sounds quite precarious. How then to go about it? We should not fear failure as all things are only mastered through personal experience, and always leave our hearts open. We must remain adaptive at all times and never succumb to rigidity. We can never have expectations of our love for there is no telling what another human being will do at any given moment. We need to always remain unattached to the idea of a person remaining in our life permanently or remaining as they were the day we met them. We can never assume we know our love, everyone has differences of opinion and secrets of the soul that may remain hidden even from themselves for years upon years. We should always respect others as we would ourselves and not stand for others treating us disrespectfully. We must be generous in gifts and love, but remain mindful not to be dogmatic and procedural with these shows as this degrades the natural flow of the relationship and devalues the shows of love themselves. We must be truthful and work to learn the tastes of the other and teach them our own. While respecting our differences we must appreciate our similarities. We need to be ready at any moment to be completely confused but never allow ourselves to be roused to anger, jealousy, hate, or envy. Lovers must converse openly and agree to disagree, ensuring that we do not suffer too much pride. We have to master ourselves at reading subtle body movements, gestures, facial contortions, pitches in voice, and most importantly the eyes. In the end it is simple: we must love fully, be completely fluid and open, fear nothing, and embrace the wild uncertainty of the journey. We must let go.

9.

Emotion

A prevalent sickness in the world is the putting of responsibility for one's inner workings on outside sources. Time and time again we place the blame upon others for our own thoughts and actions. We get cut off in traffic and become angry and blame the other driver for our anger. We lose a loved one's attention to a stranger and become jealous and we blame them both. But no one makes us feel angry, jealous, fearful, unhappy, etc; we make ourselves feel these emotions. Likewise no one forces our hand. When we say, "Look what you made me do", or "They made me do it", this is a bullshit excuse. Can another really force us to do anything apart from physically controlling us? Of course not.

    Now it may feel as if we are forced into action at times but this is simply from the amount of unchecked power we give our emotions in ruling us. Let's go back to the scenario of driving your car when you are cut off. Here we are heading perhaps to work or to a friend's when suddenly we are cut off and we become enraged. Now firstly, why do we become enraged? Were we in a hurry and this has slowed our progress? Were we affected by the rudeness of inconsideration? Was it perhaps that we value our health and we feel the other driver endangered our well being? We do not have to allow ourselves to fall prey to the mindless control of rash emotions. At the moment we are cut off we have the choice of whether or not to be affected emotionally and then whether or not to allow our emotions to direct our actions.

    This is true of all situations. If someone has made us mad, we can stop and consider what it is that has allowed their action to be interpreted in such a fashion that we allow ourselves to feel justified in feeling angry. We will see the root of the emotion not in our adversary but in ourselves. Here we see that it would be ridiculous to even consider striking out in any manner at anyone but ourselves. It sounds like a tiresome exercise but when put into practice as a habitual mannerism we become fluid in our immediate self-reflections to such a degree that we do not even have to think about it. It becomes a natural reaction when we feel the upsurge of an unwanted or harmful emotion.

For anger at someone we may trace back to our own pride; jealousy to our dependency issues; sadness to our lack of inner strength. This is by no means a comprehensive list for everyone. We all react in different ways to different stimuli for different reasons. It is up to each of us to realize in what way we are affected and to make the necessary adjustment to our own natures. There is no universal answer.

It is not just negative emotions that are attached by the mind to outside sources. Happiness is far too often maintained in this manner. Some of us cannot be happy without a new car and new clothes, some of us must have a crowd of friends to surround us and so on. How absurd is it, to center our happiness on something in which we have no control and that will leave us wanting?! With this attachment to others and objects, we tend to develop fantasies about how things will turn out in the future because of the past or just from wishful thinking. Then of course, we are let down and we are unhappy and confused as to how this all happened. There is no need to be cold and indifferent to things that make us happy or that we enjoy, but there is also no need to become attached to a desire for such things. We need only enjoy what we have while we have it and then ensure that we do not obsess over it or have expectations of it in the future.

Now there are invariably some of us that say that to deny our emotions is to deny our humanity. This process of controlling our emotions does no such thing. It leaves the realm of feeling open to us as humans, but controls the direction and timing of our emotions to better suit our needs and allows us to be in a constant state of contentedness. But to some, controlling and directing of our emotions alone takes away the human essence of those emotions and thus makes them false and rather inhuman. Why is this so? Is it unnatural for man to control his nature? Since the earliest of history have we not altered our surrounding nature through architecture and agriculture? Have we not also clothed ourselves and groomed our outward appearances? Would it not be just as natural for man to groom and alter his inner nature as well as his outer?

To this, some will retort that although we may control outward things and bring them under our control, to do the same to our emotions would effectively kill the drama of life which defines human feeling, the crests and troughs of emotions. The rage of a fight, the humiliation of defeat, the kiss of lust all washed away by a universally bland state of un-movedness. Let us respond as such: where we have felt an emotion before ourselves, we are able to engage in empathy and feel for others while not personalizing the feeling at all. In this way we still find it possible to feel the breadth and depth of human emotion while not actually succumbing to its driving effects. There is no blandness when we are able to feel degrees of contentedness and happiness. There is no reason to fall into negative spheres of emotion. If we focus the attention we previously had upon the negatives and focus them on more positives, we are in effect only rearranging our routinely accessed emotion while not at all forgetting what we have felt before. Here you are still experiencing a range of emotions with just as much attention as before without being dragged to the depths. We can imagine our feelings as a linear graduated scale with the worst of our feelings at the bottom and the best at the top. Most of the time, our feelings jump about uncontrollably throughout the scale. If, rather then letting them jump about positives and negatives, we instead focus our effort on the positive half of the scale while maintaining the same amount of awareness, we are in effect retaining the same range of feeling, in that now the force of attention dedicated to our emotions in the top half has doubled and therefore the lower positive emotions are given the same depth of feeling that previously our worst negative emotions had retained.

      In the end describing the state of mind in which we have control over our emotions will always sound a little odd to those of us that don't practice it. Then again how do we describe what it is like to eat our favorite food and the way it tastes to someone that has never eaten anything that remotely resembles it? It is impossible! Experience can only be understood through direct experience. The great thing about food is that if we don't like it, we don't have to eat it again. The same goes here, we don't have to control our emotions but we can try it and we can always go back to our old ways of being controlled by our emotions. We should never mistake feeling contentedness for blandness. We generally assume if we are not feeling great and we are not feeling horrible we feel nothing. This is a dualistic mindset and is a false supposition. Just as God is and is not, is both and neither, we should consider contentedness in a similar fashion.

The spectrum of human emotion is contained by opposite polarities: Love and Hate, Fear and Fearlessness, etc, another of the many colorful instances of duality. The emotions we go through and the actions derived from them form the dance of humanity celebrated in theater across the ages. It is funny that we can observe the actions of actor and actresses as absurd or overdone, yet when we find ourselves in similar situations in our actual life we do not act much differently! This human theater is nothing more than stage-less playacting where our cues are not from a director but from the social and personal programming we have received. Here our fellow actors are just as oblivious to the fact that we are all marionettes following our programmed actions thus making us, the actors, a convinced audience as well.

When we center ourselves in the ever present moment and dis-attach from the past and future, when we cease to seek joy from the outside but find truth and light from the inside, when we find the blissful nature of that unending moment and understand the interrelatedness of all things, then there is no need to seek fulfillment outside of ourselves. All things are contained in the source, and we being of the source, all things are contained within us.

Evil

Good and evil are completely subjective concepts. There is nothing so simple as black and white. There exist myriad shades of gray. When we talk of evil the first thoughts that come to mind are of murderers, rapists and sadistic monsters. But evil also exists in a far more subtle and widespread manner. The evils above are but those of the polar extreme, while everyday we are involved with the subtleties of evil. What we speak of here is the wickedness of man, the self-centered drive to fulfill ones desires at any cost.

Oddly enough we find this concept of inconsideration and self worship idolized in our culture under the politically correct term ambition. Ambition is celebrated in an industrialized world where success in business is the highest prize regardless of the cost in suffering it inevitably creates. We find that productivity and profit is held higher than human dignity. In such a scenario ambition turns from being a vice into being a cherished personality trait.

Simply put, ambition is not something to be celebrated but to be considered a sin. Although what we term progress is not in itself an evil, nor those of us that humanitarianly help it along, those of us that would put to suffering and injustice our fellow man for the sake of greed and pride are indeed following evil paths.

We take for granted the systems in which we grow up in and assume that they are in the right and often as being the only possible way for us to live. This assumption is from lazy mindedness, another sin, sloth. We grow up seeing our parents and elders doing things a certain way, we perhaps rebel as teens and demand change, then when we have children of our own or find ourselves low on funds, we decide to play ball and partake in that favorite pastime, selling out. We become dependent on the status quo for our food and material needs. Instead of attempting to change the system from within, we seek the easy way out, just going along to get along and soon we become fully that which before we hated. We justify this under the guise of survival when in fact it is out of fear of poverty and fear of our pride being hurt. As simply as that, our society stagnates until it lies on the brink of collapse. From the ashes of collapse will rise a new society which evolves to its own peak through brave minds and efforts until again corruption seeps in and honor and freedom are replaced by fear and domination and we then fall again.

      Currently we are in the corrupted phase of social evolution where fear, self interest, and domination thrive. Any ideas that do not serve to further the strength of and dominion of the status quo are subverted and suppressed. An instance of this oppression is found in the redirection of the frustration of children with society by focusing and controlling them in the form of anti-smoking campaigns and voter registration campaigns or going green. This effectively destroys the social unrest of teens and young adults by convincing them that they change the world by working for the corrupted system rather than against it. Of course this is all a ruse to control those that are full of angst but are not mindful enough to observe the actual causes of ill in society. Effectively this does nothing to enact real changes but rather only those changes already decided upon by our controllers.

Of course there are those of us that are not taken in by such obvious ploys by the elite to stifle social unrest and are well aware of the corruption and anti-humanitarianism webbed throughout our society. One solution in place to suppress any further growth in the numbers of awakened masses is two pronged. The first attack is to censor the media; in effect, the media simply ignores and does not cover real pressing issues. This way the general public that is unmindful may not become educated and question what is going on. The second assault happens when the media can no longer ignore the riots, blogs, videos or demonstrations. When this occurs the media assigns negative terminology and demonizes the demonstrators. This causes the general public to turn away from the explanation as to what is going on and rather to side with the media analysts and experts out of patriotism and/or extremist morality. The terms used in demonization are anarchists, libertarians, constitutionalists, violent demonstrators, rioters, extremists, terrorists, psychotics, religious zealots, etc. These words in conjunction with carefully controlled footage, or lack thereof, effectively neutralizes any possible backlash by the public pertaining to the events that caused demonstrators to act up in the first place.

This is just one example of the tools which are used to maintain stability / stagnation by those that would rather compel us toward productivity and dominion through distraction than to allow our human dignity to reign at the expense of their profits.

But what is meant by dignity? Human dignity is a vague concept. It is the ability to hold our head high while not looking down on others as subservient or looking up at others as if they were upon a pedestal. Dignity is to regard others as free in their actions and ourselves free in our own so long as we do not outrightly harm the basic needs and INHERENT freedoms of another. This does not encompass disagreements of taste but upon infringements on basic rights such as freedom, property, survival, etc. For a society to force the majority of us to work as wage slaves while business owners live in huge estates and do little work is undignified. The sharing of our food or clothing with another out of compassion and friendship while not trying to get anything out of it in return but our mutual happiness, this is dignified. To be open to change and flow with the course of human nature as opposed to forcing our humanity into a conceptual mold is dignified. There are countless examples but this will suffice to give a picture as to what is referenced here as human dignity.

    Men of ambition, seeing that the most efficient means for them to gain material wealth and social stature is to utilize other men as replaceable cogs in their profit machine, embrace the system of industrial domination. Those that are courting the system for self gain have no interest in reversing its negative effects on the dignity of man and seek all means available to subjugate the rest of us more efficiently for use as mindless drones. Rather than an idealistic upper class of philosophic and religious rulers and a lower class of respectable and moral tradesmen, we have an upper class of rich malcontents bent on subjugation and total control who are self absorbed and treat anyone not as wealthy as them as lesser beings, and a lower class that is made unwise, ill educated, superstitious and amoral through it subjugation.

    Gluttony, greed, sloth, and pride, these are characteristics of the ambitious man and they have a widespread effect on society. Like a domino effect, a small corruption is introduced on the system like a virus which then spreads and grows and if unchecked will destroy the host. It is the duty of all men who live in a society to remain vigilant against any corruptions in their society that are affronts to human dignity. It is not our duty to perpetuate evil or to turn a blind eye to the suffering of our fellow human beings. It is not our duty to profit. If there were a list of our duties, chief among them would be to achieve an experiential understanding of God, and to improve the lives of all our family, humanity. These duties are impossible to fulfill when we allow our society to focus on the destruction of human dignity and the idolatry of materialistic gains.

Selfishness is the virus, the corrupter. This selfishness comes from attempting to fill the hole in one's soul incorrectly. It is impossible to fill this hole with anything but the divine light and love, whatever your religion may be. Yet we find ourselves trying again and again to fill ourselves with "stuff". In corrupted society the prescribed filler is money and power, but as we have all seen in everyday life, when those of us who are power or money hungry get what they desire they only feel driven to get more and more. It is the ancient concept of the hungry ghost. For those unaccustomed to this concept consider the following: The hungry ghost is an allegorical creature who has a large distended stomach and a tiny itsy bitsy throat. The hungry ghost is always devouring food, but it never gets to his stomach. He is never full. He is constantly seeking future food rather than enjoying what he has at the moment.

Evil is not inherent in all men but becomes inherited by all, when too few of us stand in the way of corruption. Evil does not exist outside of society, therefore if we are to continue to live within society should we not endeavor to make society exist without evil?

11.

Hungry Ghost

It is ill-advised to be a hungry ghost. What can be done to avoid this condition, or if suffering from this condition, how do we escape its grasp? The initial step is to be self aware. We must be able to observe our actions and identify the repercussions. If we come to realize that we are constantly seeking fulfillment of our desires and that we are never fulfilled and the desires only grow larger, then we must decide if we would like to change our habits or maintain our present course. Should we decide to make change then we must have the strength of will and mind to look into ourselves for the cause of our hunger, our desire. This is where it gets tricky, for the mind is a very murky place for most of us. Delving deep into this torrent of thoughts, ideas, and feelings is rough traveling especially if we do not have a direction or known goal.

Where do we begin to look? Begin with the desire. What is it? Why is it so tempting? Where does it originate? How is it supposed to fulfill us? Let us suppose that we have a driving addiction to being the center of attention. This may originate from being ignored when a child or perhaps being paid much attention while younger and then being consequently ignored for a great length of time we when are older. This could in turn form ideas within ourselves that we are unworthy of affection or these ideas may cause us to feel that we must be befriended by everyone we meet. Let's assume for the sake of brevity that we were ignored as a child and feel we must befriend everyone. We depend on the attention of others in order to feel happy and in order to reinforce that we are a decent person. When we are not receiving attention we feel as if we are empty and are unhappy. No matter how much attention we receive as soon as we are alone again or ignored we feel worse then before. We attempt to be surrounded by other people as much as possible, we are always boisterous and acting out. We attempt to convince others that we are the best, the coolest, the most fun, the happiest in order to convince people to be near us at all times. At the same time though we remain distant in regards to our feelings so that no one may find out how insecure we really are, for although someone may help us get to the root of our problems, it would possibly ruin our ability to be the center of attention and that is not worth the risk!

Here we have the desire, its origination, why it fulfills, and why it never sustains fulfillment, leaving us just as empty as before. Now that we have understood this information and it's interconnectedness we must proceed to the questioning of desire. Why do we desire? What is it we are attempting to accomplish? What we will find is that at the root of desire lies an emptiness, a need to be whole. In this instance we are seeking to fill our void with external appreciation and respect. These are two different aspects of love. Therefore we are looking to fill the whole inside of us with love from external sources. Why then are we seeking love from outside? We feel unable to love ourselves because we feel incomplete. We end up with a vicious cycle where we seek love from others but are unable to reciprocate or fully embrace love because we feel inadequate. Constant seeking leads to constant self-defeat, which leads back into constant seeking. What then is the cure?

Rather than depending on outside sources of which we will never fully trust anyway, we must come to terms with our problem for what it is. We must love ourselves. No one from outside can convince us that we are perfect as we are and that we can rest easy. In the end even if someone tells us that we are a good person and we concede to agree, WE are the active ingredient in convincing ourselves, NOT them. It is up to ourselves whether or not it is justified. So, this is it: We must tell ourselves that we are indeed a fine person and believe it! It is really quite simple. We cannot depend on the external for our internal welfare if we are to remain happy with our lives in the midst of an ever-changing world.

  This was just one example, but through this we now have a general idea as to how to go about self-diagnostics and tune-ups. Whether we are addicted to attention, profit, sex, or collecting dead dried-out frogs from under every couch we find, this method will put us in charge of ourselves and with the help of strong will, rid us of our demon the hungry ghost.

  If we find ourselves struggling with how to justify to ourselves the change needed, regardless of our chosen desire to fill our emptiness, we need only contemplate deep inside the Self upon The Source of all that is, and our relationship to It. When this relationship is understood, there is no need for dependency on any external sources for justification or contentment. Call it the love of Jesus or the contentedness of Enlightenment, call it purple snuffalumpagus if you want, it doesn't matter. It is yours for the taking so long as you look for it.

12.

Youth

Remain young. Seriously, I mean it. Do not assume this means to remain physically young by always eating healthy foods, getting plastic surgery, working out every hour of the day, or remaining mentally and spiritually ignorant. Sure a youthful body is nice, but what are you going to do with it when you die? Absolutely nothing. I find it quite disturbing to consider a life wasted in the sole upkeep of a body, never tasting rich foods or risking injury. We are built to age and built to break and heal. We ought to embrace our nature rather than shun it. We should have moderation in our food and drink, our rest and our exercise. We can enjoy the fruits of existence, while not being gluttonous. Also on the note of mental ignorance, we shouldn't assume it charming to remain immature, selfish, inconsiderate, etc…it isn't.

When we speak of remaining young we mean to remain open, like a child that is new to the world sees everything with fresh eyes. A child that has never seen something or someone before has no expectations; neither should we. We must always be open to the idea that we may learn something new, and regard our past knowledge not as something of our own to hold sacred but as something which is but a piece of information unattached to who we are as a soul. Therefore if we are to come across a contradictory piece of information we are not guarded against it as if it were an affront to who we are as a person. We must not identify ourselves with a culture, a society, a family, a team, a race, a color, a religion, etc: our soul is unchanged by these things; only our facade of self, our person, is affected by them. We should therefore maintain the relationship of self to soul as a newborn, rather than self (personality) to exterior sources.

The concepts of duality and separateness are passed on to us from our elders. When we come into the world these things make little sense and seem quite absurd. This harkens back to the Devil and the illusion of our separateness from God. The time of infancy and childhood is spent being convinced of the separateness of all things, taking away our gut instincts of the interconnectedness of existence. Go back to your infant mind and that gut feeling for it is right and true! Yes, the illusion of separateness exists, but that does not void the reality of interconnectedness in the world.

This takes us back yet again to our understanding through language. Language teaches the child that a thing is a name, and this name is separate from another name. This does help in the areas of science and industrious labors but with no cultural indicator strong enough to combat this isolating factor, we begin to feel separated from all things. We should try not to think in words; in fact we should attempt to not even think but to act from instinct. This does not mean act from habit. We must learn to differentiate the two. Instinct is unlearned and is to consciously flow with nature while habit is to act subconsciously out of repetitive patterns of action. We must not categorize the world around us but rather realize our interwoven existence with that which is outside of our person.

We cannot focus on the future or the past, but must remain constantly in the present. Children, living so much in the moment, see mere moments as lasting for hours, and hours for days. They often crave something which they had enjoyed and are at pains about it for they feel as if they will not see it again for aeons. We though, by having lived life a bit longer, understand that things come and go and come again. We are therefore at an advantage over the child in our ability to not suffer desires of the past and future. The trick is to become dis-attached to that past and future. Why should we let a youthful mind be wasted only on the young?

War

In all that is spoken of wars old and new, there is one thing we can know for certain, much of what we know is constructed of lies. "When the rich wage war, it's the poor who die." This quote from Sartre cuts to the heart of the issue. History taught to the public softly brushes aside the influences of business in war, while modern media blatantly ignores them and incites blind patriotism in the general public to justify any military incursions. War is fought for power and money. War is not fought for a clash of ideals as the theory we are forced to swallow would suggest. War is an act of business. The men who run governments are businessmen themselves or their public offices are effectively owned by business. Either way, it is business that sends a country on the offensive to secure or destroy materials, minerals, production facilities, roads, harbors, oil fields etc. Likewise it is business that amps up defense of a country on threat of invasion so that the profits of industry leaders are not taken over by others. It is not patriotism or humanity that drives big business to war, it is self-serving greed.

It is far too difficult to slaughter an entire populous and repopulate the area with a different people. What is most likely to happen on conquering is for the working class to be left in place while the upper crust is overthrown and replaced with foreigners or puppets. This of course leaves all standing industry in place so the new government does not risk an uprising from a starving general populous whose numbers far exceed that of the standing army.

This is where the concept of patriotism comes in to play. As is readily apparent, wealthy self-serving men are not likely to give up their position of economic or social stature. They are not happy to be put to death, exile, or worse yet, poverty. Just so, regular men are not willing to give up peace and prosperity for their families for the sake of self-serving masters. The most effective means to mobilize a population behind the wealthy is not to tell them the truth. Instead what is done is to convince us that others outside of our borders are blood thirsty, uncivilized, and sadistic. We are told that should any foreigners ever take hold of the homeland under military might, everything that we hold dear will be lost.

This sounds like much work but it is rather simple. Simply brainwash patriotic values on youths in the guise of public education. If that isn't enough, through media and religious agencies we are taught that the foreign devils are godless and wish to slaughter all unbelievers. Next, suppress all information to the contrary. This is not very hard to do when we have brainwashed believers in government and media positions who casually throw out contradictions to their opinions as outright lies.

Wars are then fought by the poor and the workers. Fathers and sons leave their families to the hands of fate as they throw on their battle-rattle and leave to fight a war for lies and other people's profit. To those that fight, this war is for their families' and friends' sake, for the sake of everything they hold sacred. If we try even to suggest to many of these men that they fight for nothing more than the sake of the wealthy and privileged, they will become enraged and defensive and we will be called unpatriotic, treasonous or worse.

Those of us blinded by patriotic lies will tell the rest of us that their duty is glorious. There is nothing glorious in the act of killing or dying in battle under the auspices of deception. If you and yours are sure to be slaughtered if you do not fight, then the glory of death in battle exists. But to die alone in a strange land or kill a stranger with a family much like your own while convinced your actions are for the good of mankind when they are for the good of a few profiteers, what is this? There is nothing honorable in gullibility or in a self-imposed and self-perpetuated state of ignorance.

Not only is war fought for the sake of preserving business and securing others on foreign ground, but evolving side by side with war has been the war economy, also called the military industrial complex. This is an entire sector of industry and government devoted to weapons, destruction, domination, and of course profit through continued warfare. It is in the best interest of these companies that wars should continue. They do not wish war to continue in the search of peace for man, but in order that they should continue to make profit. If war were to cease or they were to create an affordable weapon that was effective in stopping war they would be out money. An instance of the war industry and its tendency towards endless war is found in the second war between Iraq and the U.S. Under the excuse of political correctness and the battle to win hearts and minds, rather than classical domination through short-termed annihilation and forced foreign dependence, the combat is now fought repeatedly over the same ground. Allied forces go in to dominate an area taking out insurgents and then fall back. Insurgents then seep back in and the process starts over again. Munitions, uniforms, training, soldiers, food, water, weapons, etc. are in a constant need to be restocked and hence the profits of the war economy continue to grow.

For what reasons would anyone condone war? Freedom and Greed.

14.

One World

Just as for countless ages governments of the world have used fear-based patriotism to rally their subjects and convince us to go to war for our masters, another strategy uses war itself as a ruse to control nations, continents and perhaps the world. This modern era of subterfuge effectively began with the first international banks hundreds of years ago. Through these banking families who traded interests and monies across borders were born the first internationalists in the modern sense. Rather than worry about their home nation conquering vast areas of land and peoples, these families observed that by investing in interests on both sides of a conflict they would be able to profit from the winner through future contracts and development but through the loser as well by bleeding them dry of investments before their fall.

For example we may find a person living in France who held investments in weapons manufacturers in England as well as Spain during their period of conflict. More recently we may find a steel company registered in the Caribbean whose interests were owned by a family in the United States selling materials to Nazi Germany while WWII raged on. Perhaps tomorrow we may look back and find terrorist groups across the globe funded by the same groups that fund election campaigns in North America. Interestingly the duplicitous nature of these internationalists has been encouraged as strategy for popular deception through governments. In particular let us consider the United States.

Originally a system devised to enable the freedom of men, the system of free elections has been corrupted by a two party system. Warned against by the Forefathers, partisan politics divides us, destroys freedom of election, and corrupts our government's duty. By dividing politics into hemispheres of opposing ideals, the dualistic mind of man is directed into the most basic assumptions that any item of topic is limited in discussion to its polar extremities. Something is either good or bad; there is no middle ground or no other option than the two opposing propositions of the two opposing parties.

By this means of polarizing opinion of the population, the hand behind government is cloaked. When something is desired by those who hide behind government, a political party picks it up as an election platform. We, being convinced that political parties and their ideals are attached to us and thereby controlled by us, concede to pile upon the band wagon of popular support in order that our collective ideal should be written into law. This of course is followed up with a large amount of lip service from the opposite party in the media about the detriment of such and such a plan and how it should not be enacted. But alas on the day of the congressional vote the bill still passes, more often than not holding many of the votes of the supposedly opposing party.

It is now quite obvious that American congressmen act much like internationalists, but rather than playing countries against each other, they instead play us against ourselves through the polarizing mirror of politics. When we tire of this masquerade and begin showing evidence that we are becoming conscious of it, or the actors in government become convinced that their theatrical game is instead genuine, an ingenious practice is employed. A massive calamity is then created in order to mobilize public opinion behind any or all parties so that peace and prosperity may be restored. Sometimes this is an economic crash orchestrated by industry and central banks, both organs of the same internationalist body. More often is the use of a false flag attack. This not only preserves control as would an economic crash, but preserves profitability and distracts public attentions away from American interests and towards a third party.

Take for example the Reichstag fire of Nazi Germany, the Gulf of Tonkien prior to the Vietnam War, and the attacks of September eleventh on the United States. Instances like those listed above enable the shadow governments of the world to more easily move about their agendas by placing them directly in the public eye, by convincing we the people that the tyrant's agenda is actually our idea. We generally assume that activities that are held contemptible by the U.S. would not be tolerated in a democratic society. Although this is generally the case, when a call to war is made and we fear for our safety and future, we become more than willing to give up our freedoms and cease to question our government's actions out of the assumption that the government knows best and that it would be unpatriotic to disagree in a time of war. These feelings are reciprocated and amplified by the media, again controlled by the same interests involved in directing government.

Before men could read, before books were everywhere and the Internet opened the world of knowledge to the poorest men, populations were more easily controlled through social structures and base emotions. Men were controlled through hunger, fear, imprisonment, dishonor and death. As the industrial age proceeded towards the information age it was necessary for regular men to be educated in order that they should build and operate the machines. With learning the mind develops skills at creative thinking and tendencies toward analysis. Men began to understand the system they were born into made them slaves while noble blood retained wealth and privilege at the cost of the rest of us. With a large population seeking freedom and creating rebellions around the world it was necessary for the would-be shadow governments to create the illusion of freedom while laying the groundwork for a control grid and maintaining their profits.

In America and then Europe the old guard was toppled, the nobility replaced by the industrious. Fueled by greed and generations of coveting, what began as the enlightened search for freedom soon became a corrupted race for economic domination. Here the Bourgeoisie, originally a middle class of industrialists, bankers, and military men, now became the new nobility. Having the power over supplies, money, and force, this section of society fought for position in government and society, inevitably winning out over the uneducated and ignorant. Rather than working to create any utopia for the generality of man, the evil men of the new nobility, entranced as they were by the wealth of the old nobility, set out to fashion themselves a similar lifestyle at the expense of the workers. It is here where party politics as it is today has its birth. Doubtless there are multiple parties to vote for on a ticket but generally all but two are ignored as irrelevant by the voter. This historical division between the educated rich and the uneducated poor continues today between the liberals and the conservatives. In most cases you will find that those with the most to lose and least to gain by any change are the conservatives, namely the wealthy. And of course we associate the liberals with the poor, for they have little to lose should any change occur for better or worse.

The two-party systems are further distorted to shape the opinions of the masses and cause disagreements within families, states, and nations and hence make men more controllable. What is done is this: Party platforms are created which oppose each other in paradox. The conservatives advise that their beliefs are in retention of wealth and smaller government in order that they should retain the vote of the rich, and then when discussing their moral values they seek to hold the vote of the puritanical and materialistic poor men who value hard work and pride, and thus the party supports the idea of free enterprise, promising the poor man that if he works hard and keeps his mouth shut he too will have riches. The liberals attract the poor by saying that they want a larger government to take more money from the rich and redistribute the wealth. Then they court the educated rich by purporting philosophical views and values like individual freedom, universal suffrage, and the equality of man.

The average mind is easily disturbed by the apparent absurdities of paradox and it is likely to fall into the realm of double think. This suffices to distract men through infighting and self-deception from the hands that hold the reigns of power. How often do we see a world leader claiming his right to invade a country because of the inherent right of his and all nations to maintain sovereignty? We hear the argument, see the contradiction, and acting under the assumption that we must be missing something we presume the purveyor of the statement to be more intelligent than ourselves because he is a leader of sorts. We thus allow the most absurd and unjustified actions to go on under our noses. Worse yet, we even support the absurdities because many of us want to be seen on the side of those in power in the hopes that it may reflect upon us and help us fulfill our own desires of greed and pride.

In a similar sense we are told in times of crisis to give up our rights in order that the government may protect us and keep us free. How terrible this statement is, yet it is true! We believe in goodness and truth. When a freedom is given up it is assumed to be a necessity we must endure for the future of ourselves and the good of our neighbors. It is rarely believed that anyone could be so deceiving, so calculating, let alone an entire governmental system so far corrupted. It is so hard to believe that when we are confronted with evil tendencies we find them so upsetting to our world view that we mentally block them out.

We end up with a system of domination that, with the use of banking, industry, media, politics, self-deception, self-denial, sin-based fear, and paradox, suffices to control the majority of the public regardless of class. Those who slip through this clenching fist end up in jail, ignored, or assassinated. All in all an extremely effective system for pulling the strings of an entire nation, perhaps even the world.

With this control over so-called "free" states, internationalist profit is inevitable. An interesting tactic is the third world development loan from an international monetary fund or world bank. First, an international bank or fund owned by our friendly internationalists shows interest to an engineering company, controlled by those same internationalists, to develop third world countries. Then the engineers go to said country and develop a plan for infrastructure, what to build and what it costs and where they plan the economy to go. The numbers now fudged and predictions filled, the write-up goes back to the bankers for approval. Their work approved, the engineers go back to the third world nation and convince its leaders to modernize and join the rest of the west. Under the terms of development it is agreed that all the international moneys spent on infrastructure must go to the already selected firm. Also tracts of land and natural resources are signed over to foreigners as well as a high percentage of the products produced by the newly built infrastructure. In effect the money goes in, builds the infrastructure, and goes out. The infrastructure built is leased out to foreigners and/or a large percentage of the profits are exported to them. The third world nation is then left with an enormous amount of debt which it cannot pay off due to the annual rate of interest being higher than the annual amount of profits it agreed to skim from the productions of its own infrastructure.

This is economic imperialism. Rather than invasion for resource control, control is achieved through trickery of the public and the collusion of the elite. When an installation is attacked and American, British, or Chinese assets are in duress, then the military of the nation to which the engineering firm belongs goes in under the guise of saving its citizens when in reality it is stifling a slave uprising. More amusing yet is when the United Nations military goes in! This is the new empire. International corporate conglomerates cutting up the pie. Instead of the excuses from the old age of empires of bringing peace, religion, and society to the pagans, we use the excuse of bringing modernization to the backwards world. In both cases the third world country is brutalized and the developed countries lie to themselves saying that it had to be done for such and such cause, never openly admitting unless behind closed doors that it was done for the sake of greed. The government, the media, the schools, the churches will send us to war with the impression we are saving our nation, our families, our beliefs. Many will return from war and tell the tale of terrible deeds done for no reason other than for belligerent control and profit. Most of us will listen out of kindness but will not hear a word our disillusioned soldiers say. It is nothing; it is hushed away as a delusion from somebody who suffers shell shock or post traumatic stress disorder. What is one soldier's tale when held against the constant social bombardment of patriotic values in the media?

Internationalists have also been working on other projects. Through the use of polarized world views and investments they have directed the formation of the European Union. At the end of the age of independent empires, Europe was composed of democratic and aristocratic states. Naturally a fight for domination arose between the two opposing forces. WWI was fought and ravaged the continent. A league of nations was proposed but the terms of surrender were too harsh on the losers of the first great war and all nations involved held deep seated anger against the others. Economic hardship in a defeated Germany brought about a nationalist zeal. Internationalists with companies in Germany eventually found in Adolf Hitler's Nazi party a refuge for business and invested in his party, seeing the likelihood that it should overtake government. More business friendly than the previous regime, and devoted to military might, soon production was again at a high and profits were returning to German business. International companies involved in the production of steel, oil, and other products began profiting by the war production in Germany. Companies who hid their actions through the use of shell corporations continued to sell to every nation that would buy throughout the war regardless of in which nation the stockholders resided.

In a similar act, the communist coup of Russia had been funded directly by Wall Street. Weapons, machinery and technology were exported by the allies to Russia. This continued during WWII as well as during the Cold War when the old ally became an enemy. Although the United States would be allowed to enforce an embargo on communist Cuba whose trade was relatively inconsequential, it would be extremely inordinate to embargo a nation the size of Russia in which such a profit could be turned on both sides. Although it was forbidden in the public eye to aid the enemy, it is quite evident that not only was weapons-producing machinery sold but the scientific discoveries made in the west were quickly and inexplicably put to use in the Soviet production plants. Some would blame this simply on spies and lowly thieves, but what is clear is a combined effort of collusion and open ignoring of potentially treasonous acts between the scientists, governments, and businesses involved. All of this was necessary for our game of opposites, the two equal super powers emerging after WW II.

WW II was set up to finally unite Europe. Europe would either fall to the Nazis and stand together opposed to the new threat of communism, or Europe would band together and conquer Germany while still being opposed to communism. Either way the internationalists would have their way when a war-ravaged people were exhausted into submission. WW II ended and the states of Europe west of the iron curtain slowly settled in a loose fellowship of mutual dependence and defense called the European Union. It took over 50 years but now the EU has a military, a central bank, and an interdependent industry. Through the deception and direction of entire nations, through war and psychology, tribes that have been fighting for centuries only now begin to recognize their neighbors as family. It is rather terrible and exciting, isn't it?

Europe is not the only Super-State in formation either. We have in Africa the newly formed African Union. Slowly recovering from the abrupt end of colonization shortly after WWII this continent had devolved into a perpetual turf war of tribes and countries. We don't culturally understand what is going on in Africa but if we look back at our own past customs and apply that to modern technology it is well explained. Think of this as Feudal Europe, it's colonization by Rome had ended, but rather than with maces and swords the Africans fight with Kalashnikovs, RPGs , grenades, landmines, tanks, planes, bombs, the whole shebang. The AU troops are sent in to quell these tribal fights in hopes to stabilize the region. If enough funding is given to troops, and enough propaganda is distributed to the warring factions it is possible that the people of Africa may grow tired of generations of war and stand at peace under a united government.

An entirely different matter is North America. Currently an effort is being made to form the North American Union. Transportation infrastructure is being built from Mexico through to Canada without the general knowledge of the public or consent of the government. A common currency has been hinted at. Lip service to border security continues as millions cross the borders unseen while driver's licenses, social security and amnesty are issued to illegal immigrants. In the United States the economy has purposefully been stunted and depressed to lower the value of the American dollar to equalize the currencies of Mexico, the U.S. and Canada in preparation for a central bank.

To what end is the internationalist conquest designed? Are we to incrementally unite the planet under a single congress and have a world capital? Is the unifying of peoples under centralized government for the sake of peace, or for the sake of control and profit? Is the ideal of a peaceful world to be dangled in the face of man like a carrot so that he may willingly become a slave? Will the world be united through the continued use of war and deception until finally there is equal peace and interdependence everywhere? Whether the outcome is freedom, slavery or in the gray area between it is far too early to tell. What is sure is that it is happening, and that we must be prepared. You say it can't be? Prove it.

15.

Time

Time is illusory, but then again so is everything else. The concept of time is created by the seemingly dualistic division of objects and space, matter and energy. By law of nature no two separate objects may occupy the same space at the same time. They may be in the same space at different times or the same time in different spaces. To anyone with common sense this sounds childish to even comment upon, but it is a necessary thing to re-evaluate the simplest conceptions of our life, for it is in these minutiae that we form our world view.

A pile of wrongful small conceptions can turn out to be a lot of trouble. We can see that time could not exist without space and vice-versa. Time is not separate from matter or energy in that neither can act or exist without time. Energy and matter cannot travel from point to point in space without time. And time cannot be perceived without a marked change in the measure or position of mass or energy. The height, width and depth of material is imperceptible without the context of space-time. Likewise energy wavelengths would be indistinguishable and unable to interact without space-time, as their peaks and troughs and intervals would be immeasurable. We have here then a complex system of interdependent dualities. In truth all this matter, energy, space, and time is an undivided and non-polarized unity. This is called the ground of all being. It is in dualities such as the aforementioned that the ground work is formed for an infinite number of possibilities to be found in this plane of existence.

We see that time is nothing but a reference between objects and space.

Time is the enabler of action. Actions sum up our existence in that everything we experience is an action. In fact experience itself is action / interaction. As there are laws, or rather habits pertaining to space-time, there are indeed habits for action in time. Actions that occur in time are of a cyclic nature. A pattern of action becomes manifested in a course of events that is repeated through history. Imagine a picture derived from fractal geometry: the shell of a snail, or a growth of crystalline structure. In fact all things in nature in some way reflect to us that they have been grown through an inherent patterned structure, some more apparent then others.

In our history the cycle of time has been represented quite often as both the Spiral and the Ouroboros. The spiral illustrates the proceeding of time from a point and how it travels outward from the source, repeating its pattern infinitely. The Ouroboros is the symbol of the snake that eats its own tail. This signifies repetition of action in time and as well as the human tendency of being caught up in chasing something which one already has, as well as striving vainly for something which has happened before and will come again in its own due time.

These symbols clearly are not complete representations of a theory as no symbol can be, though they give us a starting point for discussion. When we perceive the repetition of a symbol we generally only imagine certain dimensions of it. For example when we apply the repetition of action in the spiral to human society it fits only to a certain degree. This can illustrate the rise of a civilization from nothing and its constant growth in various areas such as population, technology, art, etc. The spiral doesn't seem though to illustrate the constant rise and fall of societies, the undulation within them. This is not that the spiral is a faulty design and it does not show us that ancient mystics were shortsighted, simply that the spiral was a simple teaching device used to slowly introduce the concept of the natural flow of time to uninitiated minds. But as we look at the Ouroboros we find that many conceptions are hidden within it. In reference to society the Ouroboros can represent the rise of the civilization out of the mouth of the snake, the course of the society as the body, the head as the corruption of society, and the act of eating itself is that corruption manifesting as self-destruction.

Just as natural life is built up and destroyed, so is the life of man. In the natural world we find land pushed up from the depths of the ocean by volcanic activity and over time its soil begets vegetation, animal life finds it way inland, and an ecosystem is developed. Then over time an invading species may interrupt and reset the balance of plant and animal life, or another volcanic or tectonic disturbance will sink the island to the depths. Similarly the civilizations of men rise and fall in a patterned manner.

Generally in a static people, a group with shared values and customs settle an area and form a governing body in accordance with said values and customs. Social classes are immediately separated in that some become leaders while others are become workers. Then a stable period exists in which the rulers and workers coexist in a symbiotic fashion. At some point, corruption seeps into the society. This happens when men become lax in their actions, when men underestimate the law and mutual respect which has stabilized their society. Fathers cease to teach sons the lessons of their own fathers, laws are misinterpreted and argued, politics split governments and churches. Business, profit, and other parasitic self-interests are lifted upon pedestals as the moral values of mutual interdependence are cast aside. With the ruling class having special knowledge and power over the workers, the workers are enslaved to whatever end the elites' parasitic tastes desire. Treated more like dogs than men, the workers become disenchanted and less productive and the material security and structure of a society dwindle. Unrest is certain. Government will likely force the population to submit and/or force them into wars with other states as distraction. The corrupted soul eats away at the body. The body crumbles upon itself, or is attacked from outside in its weakened state. Either way the civilization withers and dies.

This is the pattern of static society, and as you can see its simplest and most essential elements may be found in the Ouroboros, or two spirals layered center upon center, as two cones point to point, the point which is the apex of society, while the outer tails represent the beginning and end of the society, and the concentration of the layered form to the apex and its dis-concentration moving away from it symbolizes chaos into order and back into chaos. The end is the beginning is the end.

Of course there are exceptions to standard static societies. In nomadic peoples it is often found that when disagreements to the social system are made, those in contempt are cast out of society unless they can benignly remain. Here law is less important than tradition, respect, and mutual survival. Therefore the evolutions in nomadic culture are slow to form while basic freedoms and rights are slow to be disinherited.

Regardless of differing rates of incline and decline, all systems are at the mercy of time. All systems: plant, animal, mineral, or human ideological rise and fall, sometimes to rise again, sometimes not. All these movements through time leave an imprint upon the next. This influence causes the development of future events to proceed from a predetermined direction along its dualistic course. This gentle hand of direction is the force which creates the cyclical nature of existence. Thesis leads to Antithesis which leads to Synthesis which becomes the new Thesis. Chaos to Perfection to Chaos, and vice-versa, across the microcosmic and macrocosmic, until all existence finds its way back to God.

16.

Delusion

We have been far too serious for far too long. Something of a lighter note feels appropriate. On one hand I am endlessly pained by others' delusions, while on the other I am endlessly amused by them. Other peoples' delusions are what cause us to suffer indignation, maltreatment, and the like. At the same time though, this psychosis causes all that comedy of life which makes being in the society of men bearable and sometime outlandishly amusing. A delusion according to my handy New Oxford American Dictionary is, "an idiosyncratic belief or impression that is firmly maintained despite being contradicted by what is generally accepted as reality or rational argument, typically a mental disorder."

What I find funny in this statement is that in observing ourselves we find what is generally accepted as reality are idiosyncratic beliefs and impressions that are firmly maintained despite being contradicted by rational argument signifying an epidemic of mental disorder! Now I would not venture to say that every person born is a mental defective. No, it is simply that we are weak and lazy creatures by nature and are much better at behaving as monsters or as sheep lining up for the slaughter, than we are at achieving our full potential. It seems a logical mind and an open and compassionate heart is far too much to ask of your fellow man. It would seem like not too much to expect, but we all know how much worth to place in expectations.

What should be expected are absurd delusions from nearly everyone we meet. For instance I know a young man that is extremely intelligent, has some of the highest test scores around, and yet celebrates his repressive religion that clings to beliefs that completely defy his rational mind. This man has not only intelligence but has a background in the study of psychology, the study of the endless entertaining strife which is self-imposed. He understands rational thought, understands the way in which belief systems are imprinted upon our minds, understands that his belief system is rife with judgmental illogic, and yet he constantly allows his logical mind to be confronted with illogical beliefs and hence he suffers an endless internal struggle. Now, there is nothing that makes this situation unavoidable for him yet he continually evades any possible solutions to this cyclic state of self-torture! He would be the type to enjoy sex and hate himself for it. Of course if his belief told him to do one thing, and his body and heart told him to do another, he would end up doing what his body said anyway and then just go ahead and feel bad about it later!

   Self-delusion is one of the most common sources of anxiety. There is no need for therapy, no need for drugs. Both of these mask what is the cause of the problem. Therapy masks the problem in that most people go and talk to a stranger and feel that they are resolving their issue because they talked to some guy with a degree. Then either the patient is prescribed medication or the patient self-medicates. Quite comical. In both cases the symptoms of the mental derangement are covered over while the self-induced mental mechanizations that cause the rifts in the mind to occur in the first place are left unattended to continue their destruction. With walls upon walls built in the mind, compartmentalizing thoughts and reigning in the power of thought by corralling and killing them, we do terrible things to ourselves as well as any who may fall across our raging path.

Speaking of raging, this brings to mind the unholy and blindly faithful religious zealot. It is both infuriating and immensely funny when someone tells us about their God who loves all and is all-accepting who then turns around and tells us that we am going to hell because we don't follow the rules imposed by their religion that they themselves cannot manage to live by. Infuriating because they are judging and condemning us based on completely illogical grounds, and funny because they are working so hard to convince themselves that there is no hypocrisy in their words that they become masters at double think. Within the course of a paragraph of speech or less they can effectively contradict themselves, acknowledge both statements for what they are, and completely deny any contradiction no matter how obvious. When listening to their speech we will either fall in lock step as good little sheep or we will argue their statement, in which case the speaker will dance around the subject eventually coming to an unfounded end in which we simply cannot understand what they are talking about anymore.

Now what is this pathetic human tendency to blindly follow? It is outlandish! It is unsettling! We can trace back exactly what happens here. Some bullheaded jackass with a strong will and who is hungry for power makes some ridiculous statements about morality and sin and social order etc. He is questioned by the people around him about his statements and he tells us that if we can't understand what he is saying than we don't deserve to live in this make-believe society. Of course those that argue for logic are outnumbered by those that are more easily managed by material-based fears who have a tendency to be on the dull side.

"You must believe in marriage or you will be a sinner and therefore we cannot befriend you and you will go to hell!" Ruling by fear is the nature of rulers who value themselves and their lives over that of other men. It is as if saying, "You are a stupid person who can never be taught or managed through logical and spiritual education, and besides, if you were managed as such then you would inhibit my ability to amass property and power!".

Here the sins of the father are indeed the sins of the son. When we allow ourselves to be debased into blind follower-ship out of needless fear and weakness of will we set our children up to follow in the same position. If the youth is to resist the belief system then the adult becomes the new bullheaded jackass and the youth is forced to move out of the society or cave in to the adult's mindset. This convincing of the youth is paramount to the adult, as any disbelief by the youth will call into question everything the adult holds to be true and infallible. Therefore the fight for survival within the mind of the adult requires that they act out with the fury of a wild animal backed into a corner. I will always put my money on the person who is fighting for survival over the person who is fighting for pride, and at this point the youth is fighting for their own pride more than survival because they are not dependent on a thought system for justifying the state of their living conditions. The adult will win out over the youth in most cases, or the youth will be banished It is much less likely that the adult will come to terms with their wrongs and contemplate new ideas with the youth.

This is how systems of delusional thought are perpetuated over great periods of time. This doesn't simply refer to familial relations in propagation of mindset but also to entire social systems as if the adult were the actual working class and the youth representative of all semi-socialized youths. After even short times, questioning basic things which are central to a society become taboo, and actions opposed to the laws based on these central ideas become crimes. "While there is a soul in prison, I am not free", and neither are you. When anyone presupposes their right to govern others on nothing more than delusional ideals, no matter how ancient or historically rooted, it is offensive and suppressive. This activity is in direct opposition to the universal rights of a dignified existence. Wild animals, that we always manage to look down on, rarely treat their own kind with same lack of compassion that we humans often treat each other with.

Massive delusion is so very disturbing and attractive at the same time, much as a car wreck. Living in a world suffering from massive delusions makes it that much more easy for a man to fall prey to his own vulgar delusions. Comparatively it is similar in action to a child that grows up in an abusive family and then abuses his own in turn. But here rather than simply repeating the error of those before us, we finds that this society- wide delusional state justifies to the individual his own personal additions, in that in most minds the society determines what is right and wrong and therefore if it is right for society at large to suffer itself so, it is also right for individual men to suffer as well.

This is all done subconsciously of course as are most concepts that are socialized into our minds. It is not immediately that most of us recognize the hand that guides our formation as citizens of a nation or followers of a faith. It is only after repeated and prolonged observation of oneself and one's fellow humans, whilst attempting to be as objective and open as possible that we begin to fathom that we are not what we may appear to be.

Our egos, or persona, are simply the accretion of personal experience and socialized belief systems. Once we begin to peel the layers of ego apart like an onion to reach the core of ourselves, the base and unalterable nature of ourselves, we find that these delusions which we so dependently clung to for safety and reassurance in actuality were weighing us down and keeping us from embracing and developing other and more positive natural attributes.

Delusions are safety nets and serve much the same purpose as does the security blanket for a child. Delusions provide our weak minds the ability to have a source of unending stability in our lives. This stability provides an anchor point to fall back upon when we feel lost; like a child in a new environment carrying his binky. We strip the child of his safety blanket at a certain age. Why do we not strip ourselves of our delusions?

This illogical mindset is the very same as the much mentioned mind of stone. This stone is our anchor and is resistant to any opposing force regardless of if that force is overwhelmingly logical and helpful.

I go back to my friend from earlier. His mind is anchored in a particular set of beliefs and he builds a wall within his mind that channels incoming data and internal processes much like a maze. Once the walls are built, the mind is automated, the decisions are made subconsciously. Information is filtered and categorized as acceptable or unacceptable to world view. Then acceptable non-contradictory information is sent directly to be comprehended while the contradictory information is subdued by illogical arguments and emotional response before entering the conscious mind. It is like a maze where two people are given the task to enter the center of the maze. One student is preferred and is given clear directions to the center while the other student is given purposefully wrong directions and of course the preferred student will nearly every time reach the center far before the other.

We find ourselves a little confused and unhappy when the unfavored student reaches the center of our mind maze first and uncensored. This happens to everyone from time to time and is quickly masked over by making ourselves feel bad for having the thought when we should be asking ourselves why we should be making ourselves feel bad simply for thinking. Thoughts that go against rigid social structures are natural to humans. It is our spiritual need to be free versus our material desires for security and acceptance that cause this particular turmoil and mental self-mutilation.

This is very much the way that our entire world view is regulated and maintained in most of us. There is very little room for growth and acceptance but much room for atrophy and misplaced hatred. Should we live an entire lifetime sheltering ourselves from experiencing love and beauty, encouraging suffering through unending self- induced pain in order to break ourselves, to tame our animal heart into an ordered and controlled acceptable prepackaged viewpoint? "My preacher says that earth is the only possible planet with life, contrary to the scientific theory, and I will believe him, and if I find myself thinking otherwise I will chastise and punish myself with guilt for being a bad follower of my preacher and a bad servant to my God!" Give me a break! There is no need for a lion tamer if the lion will tame itself.

Delusional world views are propagated by society in order that it may maintain itself, one aspect of this propagation is the encouragement of the individual that the more we self-prescribe our own socialization the better a citizen/follower we are. When a western child is seen to be dressing like adults, calculating money, or otherwise wasting his youth, he is celebrated, while those children that follow their instincts to the contrary are punished and often literally medicated for being too wild and told to be more like the youthless child. Here the sins of the father are passed to the son before the youth even develops philosophical thought and can differentiate material and spiritual needs! As expected, most children concede to the adults out of dependency-based fears. This of course is quite understandable, for how is a child to know better? This though is no pattern to follow through the course of our lives, to be constantly driven by this basic programming only to develop a complex system of delusion.

We must toss away the security blanket for we do not see how it is tangled around our necks and is slowly taking our lives. When people say, "I lost everything I had and it set me free", giving up on a grasping world view is what they are alluding to. Some who say this lost their family in divorce, or their fortunes, or their physical abilities. A Rancid lyric states the following, "In a man's life he will take a fall but how low he goes it just depends." It is not the quantity of loss in the fall that is important, but the quality. It is important that we recognize the fall for what it is and that the proper attention is given to the initial reasons of the fall. Some of us will fall from millionaire to ruin and it will never phase our wickedness. Others will fall from being in an unhappy relationship to being alone for the first time in years and it will be enough for us to crack and evaluate ourselves, our life, and our world view.

We do not have to wait for the walls of our fantasy castles to crumble in order realize and fix the weak foundations in our heads. It is simply an action we must decide is valuable enough for us to spend time implementing. Internal observation and the will to make concessions and alterations is all that is needed to prevent a potential system-wide collapse of our delusions. We will find that as we chip away at the stone conceptions in our minds and the mortar of will that binds them, the castle of self does not disappear but simply takes new form. With work our Self will be as a waterfall, always present but always moving, always changing. Static while unstatic.

The waterfall symbolizes the ceasing of the dualistic mind set, that opinion that something must be one thing or the other. The paradox of the ever present / never present waterfall represents the true nature of our mind, our bodies, and our spirits. Rather than face up to the reality of the illusory nature of existence, we compensate for our illusion with delusion! This can only be explained through irrational fear.

This irrational fear is based in the view of ourselves being dependent upon social structures to define "Who I am," and upon socially acceptable world views to define "What I am". Seeking to define ourselves through such secondary measures is like comparing our hair color to a picture on a bottle of hair dye rather than just observing the actual hair!

What is important is that we cease to seek comparison to social standards or other people at all, whether regarding something so trivial as physical appearance, or something more complex like education or political views. What is most important is that we should look far within ourselves for answers to our true nature rather than place importance on the outer material world.

We cannot ask ourselves, "Am I a good child to my father," rather we must ask, "Am I who I feel I should be?" If we are in contradiction to our father's wishes, perhaps he has reasons for us to change that would be good for us to listen to, or perhaps he is a rotten father. It is up to the sound and practiced judgment of the individual to evolve one's own mentality.

While we are naturally dependent upon the love and affection of others, it is of dire importance that we truly love ourselves before seeking to develop relationships. A love/hate relationship will become readily apparent when the relationship becomes more centered upon dependency than the sharing of loving thoughts and actions. For healthy relationships, the delusional state of mind which focuses an importance on exterior factors must be expelled. When false importance is placed upon exterior factors we become addicted to them for pleasure and we lose the ability to self-soothe.

Clearly it is very nice to hold another's hand and snuggle up next to them, yes. But when someone is angry at us and withholds their love, if we are far too focused on external input, we will become distraught. Worse yet, at times we become expectant of a formulaic and predictable relationship. When a dependency on people having perfect agreement to our thoughts or wishes forms, we are left utterly confounded when our expectations are ceased to be met.

Delusions are simply poor assumptions that grow. As organic beings we tend to replicate and repeat not only our physical processes but our mental processes as well. We should not feel bad for suffering our own delusions for it is only in mistaking learned information for truth that this happens. For most of us there is no class in school, or friend with sufficient knowledge to guide us from making this initial mistake in judgment early on in life. To conquer our delusions, to chip away at the mortar of the dark castle, we only need to begin with admitting to ourselves that we are not perfect and that it is OK, or that we are perfect in our imperfection! I prefer the latter.

There is another kind of delusion though that is just as deadly as delusion learned through exterior information and this secondary form is created out of pure imagination. Imagined delusion is much more disturbing than the former. Here we find ourselves so very isolated from reality through defense mechanisms, social ineptitude, and general poor judgment that we end up nearly completely contorting all inputs to our brain mazes. So massive a defensive network of filters and walls has been put into place, that we live in a dream-like state. This delusional state may not distort all things that come into contact with our mind, but an excruciating large amount of various offensive inputs are transformed within the mind into conceptions entirely devoid of their innate meaning. This does not necessarily mean that we are severely mentally disturbed in that we will see things physically different than they truly are, but here the suffering is just as bad as we may turn all things that contradict our views of ourselves and the world around us into completely neutral ideas or worse yet those that are supportive of our disturbing mindset.

This reminds me of an officer I have recently come into contact with. This man appears to be around fifty years old. When talking to this man countless people are struck by his immense lack of social skill. In conversation he will bring up the most ridiculous statements and questions that vary randomly from being attempts at being funny to suddenly being serious, though he appears to never fully understand either concept. He will lash out when someone reacts, opposing to his ineptitude and clear mental self-isolationism, yet he will then simply approach someone new and immediately begin, undeterred along the same path of self-delusion obviously unaffected. Here is a man that for various reasons has never been able to develop social skills and has instead opted to adapt through mental self-mutilation so that his lack of relationships may go unobserved to himself, rather than identifying and adapting his own faults.

But this is only one of the more extreme examples. Most of us can witness similar activity every day in ourselves or our friends. The most common delusion is that of replacing the actual experience of another person with that of an imaginary ideal. Here the mother doesn't see the child as a genuine person but as her project to be formed into an idealized adult, the father sees his son as living for the father's unattained and idealized dreams, the woman sees her husband as being not fully formed but alterable into her own perfect imaginary husband. Just a few instances, but you get the point.

In any event, when we are the idealist, we severely suffer pain when it is evident that the focus of our imagination is not playing along. When the perfect son of the mother is expelled from school or the son of the father quits the football team to follow his own dreams, or the perfect husband to be raises the flag of individuality against his wife, those of us with these delusional mindsets lash out. This is easily observable by the extreme amount of anger focused upon the idealized person by ourselves.

After a our delusional minds have convinced ourselves through so many self-deceptions that our world view is valid, anything that is too alarmingly obvious to ignore through normal means of denial and filtration is dealt with by a burst of defensive rage in attempt to change the exterior circumstances in a last ditch effort. The cornered animal lashes out in self-defense.

If this outburst is enough to affect exterior circumstances to play into our delusional mindset, the memory of the outburst will be lessened in the our mind sometimes as much as to be denied completely, as the acknowledgment of this outburst would in turn force us to acknowledge the disagreement between reality and the delusional perceptions we hold. If this outburst is not enough to change the oppositional circumstances, then we are likely to fall into a state of depression until we are able to either confront and reconcile our issues or we have managed to reprogram our delusions and add thicker layers of denial.

It is easier sometimes to deny self-evident truths than it is to admit that we are wrong. When we realize that we are not dependent upon external sources for our internal perception of self, we cease to grasp for the intangible fantasies created in our minds and attachments to material things. By freeing ourselves from the duty of determining right and wrong and allowing ourselves instead to simply be as we are in the everlasting moment, we find that we are no longer in defense of being wrong nor do we strive to prove others wrong so that we may be right. We simply are at liberty to exist and respect the liberty of others to exist in kind.

17.

Ego

Ego, self, persona. This stuff is way too complicated. This subject is too deep, too pretentious... But you see it really isn't at all. Call it what you will but the self is not complicated nor is making careful observation of it or working to understand and develop it. Our generation has grown up in a culture that puts more value on material wealth and social vanity than on personal growth and finding our inner strength. So when we call a subject deep it is not that it is a complicated mystic or theosophical issue that is reserved only for the genius, rather it is that when we call something deep our society has heaped such a mound of detritus and excuses upon a subject that it becomes painful and difficult to dig out!

We bury issues under so many layers of social and personal denial and forgetfulness that we forget they are issues at all or even that they ever existed. We may be sitting in conversation with another when the subject changes from sports, to the news, to shopping, to church, then perhaps to something more "deep". When this occurs it is not that something that is impossible for the mind to contemplate has been brought up, it is only that our minds are not used to thinking in a particular fashion and so we become uncomfortable.

This is much like what happens when you see a family member naked or get a sex talk from your parent. The mind has developed standards of etiquette and these are also walls in our mind maze. When something that has been built up as an expectation is broken; such as never talking about sex with your mother or father, our mind reels back and we quickly must decide whether to jump into the torrent of uncomfortable abnormal thoughts, or to shore up its walls with fresh construction. It is the very same thing with thinking "deep thoughts". Consider God, death, the meaning of life, infinity, spirituality, energetic vibrations, ghosts, fortune telling, comparing theoretical particle physics and eastern philosophy, or relevant social and economic structures for a world progressing into a post-nation state era. Thinking on these subjects, though at times intricate, mental work is in reality no more taxing than anything you do at work or school everyday. The difference is only the amount of attention spent.

Are you good at working on cars, or computers, or treating humans medically? Chances are for most people that we are not good at all of them if any, but we know that anyone through a proper mindset may become a master mechanic or a computer wizard or a doctor of high ability. It is in the exercise of the mind on a particular issue that allows us to build the mental muscles necessary for concentrated and extended effort in a particular subject matter or way of thinking. So it is simple, if we are troubled by the daunting attributes of deep thoughts, yet we feel we should figure out why some of our friends can't seem to shut up about them, all we need to do is start looking at the issue in question and then all of a sudden our uneasiness fades away and is replaced with curiosity, our zeal for self-denial is replaced with the lust for knowledge.

The issue isn't deep; it is just buried in your thick skull. The issues of self are only complicated by ourselves, so why don't we just un-complicate things? Confront the issues. What is the ego? Who are we? What are we? Are we?

I have read of corrupted ancient men worshiping themselves in temples, replacing gods with idols of themselves. Currently we do much the same thing though not in the same style. We make offerings of ourselves in the form of fancy cars and bigger houses and expensive watches. We adorn our lives with flashy things so that others may see how great we must be. Many of us even talk so much of ourselves it is as if we are trying to convert others into our church of self-worship! I would argue that many religions are misguided, but this would have to be categorized as a false religion if ever there was one. Why so much fuss over ourselves? So much time is spent in offerings to the self yet we never look to see what it is we are covering in material wealth and gathering social esteem for. Perhaps we are attempting to cover up something. What would you suppose that to be? I would propose that we are trying to hide the fact from ourselves that the ego, the I, the self, is impermanent and that the you that is "you" will die. Trying to cover up the impermanence of the ego with material things is like trying to make firewood inflammable by throwing gasoline on it.

"You are not you, you're me," and "It's my body you've got there and I want it back." Those were lines from a favorite Sci-Fi movie of mine, Total Recall. Why the hell am I quoting the Governator? It's like this. You are not you, you are God, and he wants his body back. The illusion of your existence, the universe, the world, and you as well, are all from God and of God and will at some point return. All things cease to exist as they once were. All things, including the particles that compose your body, are in constant flux and transition from one state to the next. Sometimes hydrogen is in a star, sometimes in a stream, sometimes in a human body. The point is that the hydrogen particle does not belong to you. You belong to the hydrogen. This phantom we call an ego or what have you, is only a temporary set of conditions that came from dust and will return to dust. The dust, of course, being the dualistic grounds of being, matter and energy. That's it buddy: you're nothing special. You can paint crap gold, but it's still a piece of crap. There is no need to decorate ourselves in order to aggrandize ourselves; we have only an illusory and impermanent self!

Perhaps we can begin to see now why there is no ego, but this does little to shirk the odd feeling that I am still here and am for that matter quite conscious of the fact. Details, details…you people are never happy. You see, this illusion of ego is caused by the ability of the mind to differentiate and categorize and calculate and conceive of time and cause and effect relationships that go beyond the realm of the normal animal mind. Somewhere along the line humans had the idea that we should give up living on instinct and being dependent on scavenging, and that we should develop our tools into a way of life, to make our lives less about the wild flow of nature and its whims and attempt to bring nature under the control of our whims. Silly things that we are, we didn't quite realize that not only do the things we own end up owning us, but that all things we created still exist within nature and therefore all of our creations only create new problems after they have solved the initial disagreements between man and nature.

Our minds evolved away from instinct and unitary mindset, to a mindset of calculating thought processes and dualistic conceptions. It was in this development where man was able to separate himself from the world in his mental equations. If it is raining and I do not want to be rained upon I may sit in a cave. If there are no caves I may build a shelter. If I am going to farm an area and I can conceive of time, I should know that I will be there a while and will build a more permanent shelter. If I am to live in a settlement with others who farm and I don't like it much but don't want to leave perhaps I will start a marketplace for trading. Simple steps are taken over the slow course of millennium and men transform the nature of their mind, and with this, their physical surroundings. After a while what before was an absurdity is now commonplace. The thought of an ego separate of nature would be absurd for early men with no tools or formal society, but who now feels at one with nature, or that their self doesn't exist apart from nature?

Our modern lives are spent in a foggy muck of ideas and ideals. We trudge through willingly enough since we do not know any better; because our civilizations are nothing but dense spider webs of interconnected conceptions for bringing about the fruition of our ideals. If a society wishes to produce goods of a certain kind then the social order is formed in such a way as to maximize the production of those goods. If a society wishes to focus on family relationships then the society is structured to bring about the ideal social and physical situation for the ideal family relationship to flourish. Societies beget societies, and as one collapses, another picks up where it left off. In our cultures there are counter cultures and countless divisions within them. We have different religions, politics, governments, morals, economies etc. There is so much distraction in our cultures from the true nature of ourselves it is no wonder we forget who and what we are. It is no wonder that we forget that society and culture and the man-made world is only a thin veil of order over what we now perceive of as the chaotic natural world.

We begin with separating ourselves from nature in agriculture, and mechanical science, and then civilization breeds the separation further in latter generations through physical separation in buildings and roads and calculated and squared and measured lots and buildings, and mentally through socializing us into being dependent upon this system of ideas for survival. I.e. if one is never raised in the wild and cannot find water to drink or forage for food, how can he leave the city or civilization at all? Our instincts are still present but we actively socialize our young so that they may ignore them or repress them. How many people when they are young honestly can't wait to work in an office or a factory for 30 or 40 years with 2 weeks off a year? It is unnatural of course and so the idea is socialized into people that they must do this or that or they will be bad people or what have you. It's all done in a sort of social subconscious act, though it is quite obvious to anyone paying attention.

    It becomes over time an unconscious assumption by men that they are separate from nature and that their egos are permanent in an impermanent world. And as would be expected the assumptions of men become the standards of society and the conception of a separate ego becomes an attribute unconsciously socialized into the minds of youths. Question the self and you question society. Question society and you question morality and nature. Question our nature and right and wrong and you question truth. Question truth and you question reality. Question reality and you question God. It's really an overwhelming train of thought if you do not normally contemplate such things, and in our collective gut we understand the sheer power of looking deep within ourselves. It is in instinctively understanding that this veil of ideas we take for true reality is hanging by the thinnest of threads that we dare not seek to answer the question of ego when it arises.

    So you see, it really isn't a fear of things like the ego being too deep for us to reach or too big for us to handle. The fear is in finding out how shallow and unfounded our presumptions are. If we are to find out that everything we hold dear is fallacious, that everything we thought we were was based on lies or untruths, then what are we? Who are we? Are we? It is better to presume that we know nothing and seek answers, than to presume that we know answers, when we in fact know nothing.

    At this moment, what do we do? We have lived our lives and our egos have been composed of socialized thoughts and ideals and abstract conceptions forming a maze of walls within our minds. Our ego is as stone. It is resistant but cracks under enough pressure. If we have allowed only a needle of truth to enter our minds, now we can use it as a wedge to pick at the mortar between the stones. Our will is the force that guides the needle of truth. Our willpower to investigate ourselves is encouraged by the truth itself. An ounce of true wisdom reassures the self that there is nothing to fear from being picked apart. It is a journey of a thousand miles started with a single step. The first step is the hardest. Once the habit is formed and in place, self-spelunking becomes our nature and can be done with less concentrated effort and eventually becomes an automated process.

18.

Communication

I don't like to think of communication as the tossing back and forth of empty words, but as the correct display and recognition of ideas and concepts between persons. If this is the definition of communication then we can see that the casual tossing back and forth of common linguistic symbols does not necessarily imply communication but can rather represents a gross miscommunication. In everyday situations we converse with strangers and friends over many topics ranging from the mundane to the fantastic to the abstract. What we rarely recognize though is that during these interactions we are making some very large assumptions.

Firstly, we are under the assumption that the people with which we are speaking consider words with the same meanings as we do ourselves. We can have and entire conversation about how we love good dogs and our counterpart may completely agree, though we may feel a good dog is a housebroken pet that fetches things and lays around while our counterpart is envisioning an ill-tempered dog that is bloodthirsty and beaten into submission. We can never assume that simply because on a surface level things appear to be uniform that they actually are. Can we know what someone sees, hears or feels? As stated earlier on, one can never know another person's true experience and as such we can not truly know another person.

So how are we to know how someone feels when we are speaking about any particular subject? How are we to know if the encyclopedia of another person's mind is similar to our own when they have spent their entire lives looking through different eyes? In truth there is no way to physically communicate our experience to another even in regard to the simplest of experiences. We cannot even truly communicate an experience to ourselves. To experience is to be aware in the midst of action. To try and communicate awareness to another awareness, either our own in the future by way of our memory or to another perso,s awareness, is an exercise in futility. This is like trying to show water what it is like to be oil by attempting to mix the two. We are all made of energy/matter and we share similar consciousness, but what separates us from the unity inherent in nature is our ego. This illusion of self separates us all from each other as if we were islands drifting in space. Though we may be able to relate through comparisons on a surface level, without a ground in the spiritual we lack the viewpoint necessary for a more true communication.

    The trick in communication is to strip bare all words to their most base and unclouded definition. Just as we strip the mind of weedy outgrowths and presumptions, we must do the same to the words in our vocabulary. When we do this we can begin to see more clearly the words of other people. If we have no forgone conclusions when we encounter a word itself, it is that much easier to see all the various concepts that someone speaking to us may be trying to convey. In using this process it is much less likely that we will go cow-eyed, become judgmental and distant, as we do when we use the lazy minded approach of having already decided what someone is saying before they have even said it.

    Let's layout a process by which we may attempt clearer communication with others. First we must let go of all preconceived notions on the subject at hand.

We can't allow ourselves to be vainly convinced that we are a master of knowledge. We are inevitably reminded in the most uncomfortable of fashions when we become prideful and tumble from our own pretend pedestals. If we do not allow ourselves be defined by what we think we know, then we do not fall and therefore we are never embarrassed when we are proven wrong. Secondly, we should not attempt to convert a person with whom we speak into seeing things our way from the start. Those of us that have ever spoken to a religious zealot or a political extremist should understand this concept. In conversations with these extremist types we will notice from the very onset that they are not listening to the words we are saying but rather looking for any loophole they can find to get their point across. This is a ridiculous persuasion yet we find ourselves to a lesser extent doing this very same thing much of the time. Thirdly, back to the words themselves. When we find ourselves opening our minds and freeing ourselves from the bondage of preconceptions, we no longer attempt to press any beliefs upon other persons unconsciously. Now we are free to study our fellow humans with clear vision. What words do they say? How do they look when they say them? How do they define these words that define their beliefs, concepts and experiences? We cannot guide another person along a preconceived path of our own construction while we are attempting to communicate as truly as possible with verbal symbols.

  There are other forms of communication of course but these are far more difficult to mention properly in writing. There are psychic, visual, and sensual communications. These can often be easier to conceive but are not without miscommunications or deceptions. How often is a curious glance mistaken for the come hither look, or a hug mistaken for an invitation for further physical contact or perhaps mistaken for being condescending? Psychically we are often mislead as well when we think we have the same thought as someone else, or when we laugh at the same time at two totally separate things. Nearly all of these instances of miscommunication occur because of our inability to rid ourselves of preconceptions.

    We can never know how fully we comprehend another person's thoughts, nor can we ever fully comprehend another person. What we can do is to strive to perceive of things as fully and truthfully as possible without filters of any kind. This may sounds like a lot of work for the sake of understanding other people but remember that the more we learn about the functions of others, the more we learn about the way we ourselves operate, and the easier our own internal understanding then becomes.

19.

Initiating Action

Initiating action can be difficult. There is always something that we wish to do but we just can't seem to find the way to begin. Most little things, most small actions come easy to us, but there are always those that seem to be just out of our reach. We may not realize it when it occurs, but our minds find the most extraordinary excuses to get around becoming involved with the simplest of tasks. The smallest problem can seem like a huge weight. It is like a boulder teetering on the edge of a cliff. We look at a problem, or a goal that we wish to attain as a huge collection of Ifs and Ors and Buts. I would like to go to school at Harvard BUT what IF this Or that occurs. I dream of being a doctor BUT I cannot because IF I do this then I will lose that. And the list goes on and on. We play out in our minds, subconsciously for some, consciously for others, every possible reason and excuse not to do something. We fill our heads with negative presumptions based on our fears and irrational thoughts, and what started as a little dream, a little goal, has become a huge and daunting boulder of doubt.

Now anyone that is not an ultra-mega-body builder can tell you how difficult it is to move a boulder by hand. But you see, the boulder of doubt in our minds that causes our inaction is not lying on level ground, it resides on the edge of a cliff in our mind. The plateau where our doubting boulder sits is a representation of our mind's tendency towards habitual action. Just as we have talked earlier about our minds falling into habits in learning and in forming an ego, our minds also have habits which they have formed in relation to action and inaction. Our past has told us perhaps that we are not good at sewing and we are terrible with bowling cucumbers at coke bottles on a beer pong table when we are too drunk to remember our names. Our past experiences with other people have affected us as well; such as when our fathers may have said we would never get anywhere or our grandmothers saying we would be president one day. All of our past experiences accrue into tendencies and habits on our part if we believe them to be truthful. If we believe that people who have told us that we are worthless or stupid were telling the truth, we will make ourselves do stupid things and we will feel worthless. If we gave up trying to learn how to fish, we will feel that we are a bad fisherman and that any future attempt to learn will be fruitless and hence we fall into self sabotage. But it can also be said that if we feel we know everything or that everyone likes us, going to the other extreme, we will not try to change our actions even if we are wrong because we will not face up to the facts.

These boulders of doubt are not stuck forever though upon the plateau of habit. What is the way to break the cycle, when the more I think about my dreams the farther away they seem to be, the more difficult to obtain? But this is the problem, isn't it? We are thinking over and over upon our previous considerations and expending effort not in escaping our negative tendencies but rather instead we are adding concretions to the boulder and increasing the size of our habitual plateau! Instead, what we should be doing is putting the same effort into leaving our negative habits behind and rolling our doubt off the cliff, so that we may break it apart and then realize our dreams that lie inside of it, like a sculpture waiting to be realized by a sculptor.

You see, the sculpture in the stone isn't just our dreams, it is our present conscious state. When we are sitting in habitual stagnation it is us. When we are excitedly moving down the face of the cliff it is us. When we have rolled so far, when our doubts have been cast off like loose shale and we have attained our dream or goal, it is still us. We are our awareness and our action. When our awareness is surrounded by a stagnant self-made world of deceptions and assumptions, it loses track of what it is, we lose track of who and what we are, as well as what we are capable of.

What do we do? We must take action! It is truly that simple. When we directly confront our self-doubt with the power of will, we can push that boulder over the edge. When the boulder goes over it is not like a snow ball that gets bigger; no, it is just the opposite. When we realize that we have the ability to overcome doubt as it teeters over the edge of the cliff, the rest of the time that it is rolling along and we become closer to our goal, the more it sheds layer after layer of self-deception and self-doubt. When our consciousness stops rolling at the bottom of the cliff and rests at a newly formed plateau of habit we will have shed years of built-up doubts that have stopped us from getting to the goals which we have set ourselves upon.

This new boulder of doubt is much smaller and is thus much more readily pitched over the edge of the next cliff. We have at this point a much purer awareness than before. Our habitual plateau has been relearned and restructured and now slopes downward towards the cliff, as we have now become more accepting of change and discovery, thus allowing for a lesser effort to be applied to the boulder of doubt when we are ready to continue to take further actions in our lives that we previously had denied ourselves.

But how to start? Earlier we spoke of using a splinter of truth as a tool and driving it with your will. What we must do is find a truth that in some way references our self- doubt or habitual actions. Wielding this truth like a lever we are then able to will into action, pushing this boulder over the edge and down the cliff. In our heart of hearts we all know and feel a great power. We all understand on a very basic level that we are capable of great accomplishments. If only we have the courage to begin on our designs, to set out in a direction, we can achieve great things.

Feel down deep the power in yourself. We must have faith in this true power and convince ourselves of its reality. We can use this power to encourage our will. When we use our will we must be stubborn like a mule to push our doubt out of the way. Once action has been initiated, it is more likely to stay in motion than it is to stop. The only thing that will stop us from getting to where we want to be is allowing ourselves to be discouraged by obstacles along the path. If we are rolling down the slope and we see a large obstacle in the way and we are frightened, a great amount of will power must be used to stop where we are going and turn around, climb up the cliff, and set back right where we were before. It is much more sensible to use a smaller amount of will to steer our way around an obstacle and continue downward towards our goal.

This is how to initiate action when we find it nearly impossible to move. You want to build a house, do it. You want to learn Italian and go see an opera in Rome, do it. You want to find the meaning of life, do it. All we have to do is start. Now you no longer have the excuse that you don't know how.

20.

Power

Absolute power corrupts absolutely. Indeed, power of any kind tends to corrupt. Power is an addictive, enchanting and seductive force. Power allows us to build bridges over great chasms and feed nations. Power takes us to the precipices of our greatest dreams, lets us explore the smallest subatomic particle and points deep in space and backwards in time. Power is a tool that when utilized with right mind and right will brings out all of the best in humanity. But this same tool is a double-sided coin just like everything else in our dualistic existence.

Power brings about the slaughter of millions and the subjugation of millions more. Power enslaves minds in fanaticism and drains the liveliness of souls through materialism. Power destroys ecosystems for profits and destroys ancient heritage sites to perverted perceptions. No power held by any man is absolute but as we well know, man need not have absolute power to reach his full potential in self-destructiveness.

Some of us are born with good tendencies while others are driven to evil. It is impossible to predict which direction a child will go. There will always be a balancing act in nature between constructive and destructive forces and it would be outright silly of us to expect that as humans we are above this natural law. There must be evil to balance good for as long as we continue to view the world in a "this or that" mindset. Some will continue to be driven so seek power for good and some for sinful purposes.

The problem that arises with the seeking of power for those of us that seek to do good is that we are in constant battle with the forces of selfishness. When we initially seek the power to do good it is the driven by our selflessness. When we are selfless we are not focused on ourselves and our own good, it is our personal desire to help others that drives us. Alternately, seeking power over others for the sake of self-interest stems from feelings of inadequacy and a discomfort with the self.

If we have the will to have power over ourselves, we will not desire to control others. This is why those of us who are not desirous of power are the most responsible when wielding the power that we have been given. Those who are selfish and destructive are not affected by the harm they do to others in their search for power. When we are driven by goodwill to seek power to affect good actions, we must steal power away from those who are of evil nature and we come under fire from their nasty tactics.

Let us say that you are a poor merchant and you wish to help the local poor through cheap housing. You manage to find a low rent empty warehouse and fund its maintenance through charity. The housing of the poor drives down the property values. Let us also say that there is a property developer interested in that area of town who until recently disregarded the building you are utilizing because the project cost / profit ratio for turning the lot into condominiums or luxury apartments was too low. Now your selfless actions that have partly refurbished this building have opened up a new course for selfish men to pursue. Let us now presume that the developer makes an offer to the owner of the building far exceeding the amount your charity can afford. What do you do? There are many ways that this could go, but this is an example of the turning point in seeking power for good that may turn us towards seeking power for evil. Now the fight could be taken to the media or the court. Blackmail or threats could be used against the developer..

The point is that an honest fight in a system corrupted by sinful forces will nearly always fail and find the victor to be the crooked party who is willing to fight dirty. The problem with our own dirty fighting is that when we try to do good, but do so by these means, we open up ourselves to become the corrupted thing we fight so hard against.   Consider again our habitual actions. When we make the jump to evil action it then becomes that much easier for our minds to wrap around the idea of evil action the next time. We say to ourselves, "Wow, that wasn't so bad, and it was actually pretty easy." Becoming corrupted is really that simple and it takes a steadfast effort to stay away from the initial actions that lead us astray, and an even stronger effort not to be carried away by evil actions should we allow ourselves to go through with them.

Let's give another example of corruption. You are now a police officer. You have busted a guy with drugs but let him go because he gives you information on a bigger fish. You keep the drugs and use them as a tool to get at the bigger fish. You bust the big fish and find a van-load of drugs and he gets taken in along with the drugs. You are at the end of your shift about to go home and you realize you never turned in the drugs from the initial bust. You could keep them for use in future operations and turn it into the property lock up, throw it away, or you could use it to make your own profit. Most of us would turn it in or throw it away. But what if you were late on a mortgage payment, what if your brother was sick in the hospital and needed expensive treatment, or your child had special needs that you couldn't afford on your salary?

Now we are not saying that it is an evil act to want to provide for your family, but look at how much easier it would be the next time to hold back from a bust. Now rather than falling on an accidental profit we are actively seeking to shake down criminals for our own profits. How long before we are in too deep and can't get out without going to jail ourselves?

What starts with intentions of doing good can quickly turn into self-serving enterprises that are harmful to ourselves and others. We may find ourselves in a position quite similar to those people that before we had abhorred. Is it forgone conclusion that we should become what we despise, or is it a choice that we make along the way? The trick is to be aware of the course of actions in which we are present and not to be pulled along unawares into dark waters. If we are mindful of the present and contemplative of where present actions may lead us, we are then able to steer our direction in life and thus may avoid such things as corruptions, evil, and sin.

To use power to do good is selfless. To seek power for self is evil. This is not to say that seeking the power to run our own lives is evil. Not at all, seeking the power over our own self, learning our best attributes and greatest faults, addressing and coming to terms with them, are great and good actions. Seeking the power over ourselves and our rights for the purpose of freedom of movement, thought, and action are also good actions and are necessary for the development of our own selves and the building of great cultures. What we speak of here in reference to seeking power for self as evil is the inconsiderate and selfish search for power at the cost of others.

What is this inconsiderate selfishness? When a man is executed that is not guilty of a heinous crime in order to subjugate people through fear. When a corporate CEO takes millions of dollars in bonuses and a pay raise while hundreds of his subordinate workers, already underpaid, are laid off and have their pensions pulled in order to keep the company afloat. When a country is invaded and a government toppled for not being business friendly to another more militarily powerful country, only then to have a puppet dictator installed against the will of the people. When one sells addictive substances purposely to addict people and reap profit. When one climbs up the corporate ladder, pulling down everyone in their way, getting people fired or demoted as it suits them, for no reason other than their own greed. This is selfishness.

Evil power and power-hunting pushes everyone that is not directly useful to you to the wayside, and uses up those that are useful until they are no longer helpful and then disposes of them as well. Good power is about relationships and constructive behavior, while evil power is about self aggrandizement, lacks true relationships and is extremely destructive in nature.

Corruption seeps into every society as soon as it is born, just as we begin to die the moment we are born. It is impossible for those of us who live in society to avoid evil and sin completely as so long as we stay within said society we will interact with those who hold evil hearts, either directly in person or indirectly through regulation or finance. The question thus seems to be not just how to seek power for good but also how to avoid being caught up in self-serving corruption.

The large majority of us usually settle into the status quo and do not seek power. This is the working class. We do not seek to run our government or churches or corporations. On the down side we do not seek the power over ourselves either. We are content to be bound to a small geographic location, do not hold opinions out of the party line, and do not seek to affect any action that may change our easy and mindless course. Get up, go to work, come home. This may seem simply an avoidance of the world of power but this very act is indeed the life-force of corrupted power. With such a large portion of a society's population disinterested in politics and power games, the powers that be are able to run rampant so long as the basic needs of the greater population are met. You see, the only power great enough to cut corruption out of a society is the general public, we the people. But if we are fed, housed, and entertained to a certain degree there is no fussing. This is obvious when we see homeless people out on the street after a shelter was shut down and we say, "Not my problem." The city may have needed funding and asked for a tax continuance, but the majority of people with jobs who pay taxes thought, " I'm not poor and I don't know anyone that is , nor would I want to , so why should I pay for these lazy bastards to have a place to sleep?". Why educate ourselves on the mentality of people different then us and perhaps find out that our perceptions are not one hundred percent truthful, when instead we can just ignore them and continue on with our way of life. As long as the percentage of the population affected negatively by power never appears to be too large at any one moment, the vast majority of us can go on living our lives in the assumptions that, "This doesn't involve me," or "That will never happen to me."

   Our self-imposed ignorance and mental avoidance of issues is the cause of the downfall of civilizations. At some point citizens of free societies stop actively participating in their self-governing and instead assume an automated governmental body to be sufficient enough to run a civilization. This unspoken malignant decision within the general public breeds the hunger for power in those with a penchant for self- aggrandizement as they see the opening for political subterfuge in the system.

The sins of sloth and pride form automated government when we become so comfortable with our society that we feel that it can go on forever without our active and organic input. Laws are written, courts and police are left to run a society in a static fashion as if mankind is not an organic and fluidly dynamic creature subject to change in desire and sentiment. Power-hungry legislators are then left to hash out the best policies for other branches of government to achieve the goal of maintaining a static and enslaving society. In this, the founding principles of a society are slowly eroded as they are no longer considered principles by "We the people" but simply "laws" written upon "living documents" subject to the whims of the government. As the power hungry seep into power positions in this static and out of control government, principles for the good of society as a whole are replaced with laws profitable to those in power regardless of their negative effects on the rest of us, so long as we remain generally unaware and apathetic.   The only courses of action to escape the powers of evil are to leave a society behind and start from scratch hoping that this time we can stop sin from corrupting the system, or we can stay within our current system and mobilize ourselves through education to rebel peacefully against the occupying force. Gandhi and his countrymen did it against an empire, so don't say it's impossible.

We cannot fight fire with fire for it only brings more fire. To try and rise against a suppressive government ruled by a few but who control millions of security forces and fight them violently with a few armed men will only succeed in dividing the working class and isolating brother from brother, adding fuel to the fire and opening more opportunities for the power-hungry to take advantage of.

It is clear that we the people must not only be educated spiritually but that we must also remain active in our government if it is not to take upon a life of its own. The highest values must be placed on individual freedoms and social stability. This is what is commonly referred to as being socially liberal and fiscally conservative. It means that we should remain free to act as ourselves in society so long as we do not hurt others and that we must maintain the infrastructure of education and material production and distribution that allows our ease of life to continue. It is in observing these principles that we the people must recommit our government. We must maintain constant awareness of our governing and raise the flag when our principles begin to falter and change instead into the concepts of living documents / laws.

It is necessary to comment upon the above statement of being socially liberal and fiscally conservative. With personal freedoms we must be careful not to be abusive to others' rights and be considerate to their feeling, while at the same time not giving up our own rights in order to appease those who are inconsiderate of us. As such, if you like to play loud music for parties, and your neighbor raises concerns over noise levels at a certain time of day or on certain days, you should take that into consideration. If your neighbor makes no fuss, do not assume that they are unconcerned, but initiate conversation with them when convenient and ask if your activity ever bothers them. Likewise, if you have a neighbor that has loud parties and you have an issue with it, it would be better to talk to them first before calling the police or making harassing phone calls, and if you do not have an issue let your neighbor know that you don't mind so that they are not worried about upsetting you.

Our personal values should not be imposed upon others. If something hurts your feeling, deal with it and grow thicker skin. If a person likes to dress in drag and you don't like it, don't look. If something is on TV and you don't like it, change the channel. Attempting to legislate taste is an exercise in stupidity. What are you going to do when you find out that your child is gay when you have disliked homosexuals and tried to rid yourself of their influence in the past? Personal choice is just that .If someone else's actions are not physically or mentally abusing us and they are not hurting us, rather we are allowing and encouraging our feelings to be hurt. Stop playing the victim.

Social liberality in close quarters relies upon communication, understanding, and moderation. Because of the amount of work necessary for the maintenance of this ideal many of us allow sloth to overcome us and are willing to shed our rights in order to make life less problematic. Why worry about talking with my neighbor when I can just let noise ordinances to be passed into law and then just call the cops to haul them away or fine them massively when they break the law? This laziness is unacceptable.

We said above that to be socially liberal we must be free to act so long as our actions do not harm another. This means that if we are shooting a rifle we don't use another person's house as your backstop, or if we decide that we want to drive a car off road, or we don't borrow our neighbors car without their permission. Just because we want sex doesn't mean that we can just walk up to someone and force them, nor should we just steal a soda from a store just because we feel like it. Just because we can do something, doesn't mean that we should.

This is the difference between a system governing us and system of individuals governing ourselves, rather than being dependent on an outside source to tell us what is right and wrong and punish and reward us, we must tell ourselves what is right and wrong and determine this through communication with our neighbors, the reward being peaceful, free and open-hearted living, while maintaining the basic government services for punishments such as seclusion and death for heinous offenders. Things like rape, torture, or senseless murder have no room in any truly civil society.

Now if someone wants to be raped, tortured or murdered, who are we to tell them they cannot? This is another difference of libertarianistic individual governing compared to corrupted static governments. When a government is given power over people, a set of standardized ideals is imposed, when something is considered immoral for not fitting into the systematic logic of the machine it is disposed of. So, when we do something supposedly immoral like helping someone commit suicide, use drugs, or even marking our bodies we are persecuted.

In a truly free society we would not be persecuted for doing something to ourselves as we recognize our body as our property. If we want to cut off our leg and attach to ourselves a robotic leg, we may do so. If we want to do drugs and our actions do not lead us to steal or murder or rape then we are left alone. If we have a terrible disease and want to die and we ask someone to help, neither of us is doing anything criminal.

We cannot legislate life. When we try, we turn out hypocritical and ineffective legislation anyway. It is illegal to do this drug, but we can get this prescribed. We cannot execute someone that has raped people in our village, but we can firebomb an entire village as a soldier for the government.

And the list goes on an on. Why give our power away for something so crude as sloth or pride? It is our power that gives the king, prime minister or president the ability to fund extremists to fight in country A against country B, while at the same time selling fuel or weapons to country B to fight against country A. It is our power that indentures servants to sugar farms so that we can buy soda and candy on the cheap. Our power enslaves others all over the world while it enslaves us as well. All because we are too lazy to hold to our own power and too prideful in the system in which we have built to hold our power. Freedom takes self-responsibility.

As for the fiscally conservative side of the matter, let us elaborate. Being fiscally conservative means many things. One is to depend firstly on private funding for social programs before depending on tax-funded and government-run programs. This ensures a local level of involvement in the care of invalids, the uneducated, the homeless and the out of work. Having local control and management of social programs ensures that those who are trying to criminally misuse these services are thwarted rather then encouraged in their behavior under the auspices of political correctness while those that are really in need are given a better level of care and treated with respect and dignity. Is an old woman who is unable to pay her heating bill better served by a local church with her friends and family involved, or standing in a line waiting for a disinterested social worker to call her number?

A large national fund and network should still be involved in the collection and distribution of a certain amount of funding but the federal government should not be involved in local policy and should not be able to withhold funds for any reason from a community as its sole purpose should be in the equal redistribution of moneys back to localities and not in the governing of them.

Secondly material production and distribution should be focused on the well- being of the population. Profits should be made in order to encourage business development but should not be made through the mistreatment of workers, the manufacturing of defective products, or other such maleficent means. If products are made for us that fall apart, are poisonous, or otherwise defective while those of us that make them are treated poorly and paid equally as badly, who profits from this but a few? This is unacceptable.

Technological and industrial advances are an arm of human evolution and will never cease to be sought after. This said, the spreading of factories, power plants and power grids, sales outlets and office buildings should be relegated to the minimum amount of acreage necessary for production capability and human comfort. Constant urban sprawl leaves behind withering and dying city centers, that rather than being left to rot should be rehabilitated. We cannot allow our power to be used for cheap and easy profits when it could be used to breathe life into a entire sections of an old inner city.

Rather than moving lazily along chasing after cheap profits and materialistic dreams we should lend a guiding hand to the shaping of the constructions of our society. Again, we must maintain awareness of our society and act together to ensure our individual and group material security. Should we prefer a cookie cutter row of cheap sheet metal factories stretching out into the fields on the outskirts of a city, or a revitalized and reconstructed industrial area of beautiful stone and glass buildings that are sculpted to fit the cityscape? How about suburb after suburb of bland and repetitive constructions versus an area of rebuilt historical homes and converted lofts in beautiful old brick warehouses? It is not enough for us to build and spread like a virus. We must put love into what we do and what we build, otherwise our growth becomes like a chaotic cancer rather than an intuitive manifestation of our better human essence.

While we remain unconscious of our social tendencies we can do nothing but follow in predetermined routes. When we become aware of the state of our society we become aware of the causes and effects inherent in it, and only then will we be in a position to take back our power. When we regain our power we can shape the world around us in every possible way.

Now let us talk of money. The flow of money should only be regulated to the extent that no more should leave the country than comes in. Exports should equal imports. It is ridiculous to shell out hundreds of millions to a third world country for cheap goods when we do not have the money coming in somewhere else and working its way back to the original consumers by way of our own production. Bartering in goods and trading in metals or other tender should be in the power of the individual and not determined by the government. The ability of printing money or extending lines of credit should not be controlled by any government other than in the case that the government is printing money from its treasury department, NOT paying interest upon money printed through a system like the Federal Reserve. Holding financial security for some over the freedoms of others is unacceptable. Acting in this manner takes away our power and gives it to others.

We spoke above of social stability and it is important again to raise the subject when talking of money. There are many towns and villages and cities all over any given nation. When it comes to money and stability of nations it is important to note that the flow of money within a nation should not be regulated and also that the flow of money into towns that are dying natural deaths, like millions of ghost towns and settlements before them, should be watched over as to not waste resources. To throw money into a naturally dying settlement is much different than reinvestment in a proven and lively city. When flooding money into a subsection of society that has already clearly rotted from within, it is like pumping blood into an arterial wound, there is no chance it will clot, it only just wastes the blood. Stability is important to society but do not mistake stability for staticity, for fluidity is important to society as it must organically represent the organisms (us) that it serves.

We see that people everyday who having lost their wills and their power, have money thrown at them. Homeless are given coins on the street and housing rather than given job training, placement and self-respect. People are given food stamps and free money and housing because they are too prideful to work in society though they are willing to take advantage of its benefits. Without the human element of will to action, the power of money is useless to solve problems and in most cases, causes more in its wake. People become dependent upon a system of welfare rather than remaining independent as we would if our system were able and allowed to dynamically reorient itself to our needs. In order for any system to flow as it should, we must be aware of our environment and use our will actively to bring about any needed adaptation. We must see that we hold the reigns of power, not some impersonal governmental mechanism

Power is will to action. All of us have power. It is never lost, only misplaced. Our society is a corrupt one and we can allow bad men to tell us how to live our lives and give away our power to them, OR we can actively take control over ourselves and our part in society to affect good. The choice lies with each and every one of us.

21.
Coincidence

There is no such thing as coincidence. All things happen for a reason. This is not to say that there is some ultimate goal intended with you stubbing your toe but rather that events throughout our existence were set in motion along a path guided between natural laws and tendencies, and will continue along this path long after we are gone. This being said, you can take back what I said about you stubbing your toe, for you stubbing your toe serves as an action that will precipitate other actions yet unrealized in our time-line. Actually you never stubbed your toe, it has always been stubbed. Yet it is both, yet not.

You see, the illusion of separate moments is the illusion we call time. Here in the life of three dimensions our awareness is trapped in a maze. We are born, we see the walls around us and slowly come to understand our three dimensional world, and that to travel through this maze takes time, dimension four. Our awareness is trapped in this maze and we eventually become institutionalized by it enough so as to believe there is nothing outside the maze. We learn that there is only yesterday, today, and tomorrow. Up and down, left and right.

In fact what does exist is one moment composed of all things in space and time. This is a hard concept to grasp for most of us, but then again we have our awareness limited, whereas the Source of all being has no problem having awareness over all things in one moment, as this thing we call God IS all things. It's a good thing that God likes to play hide and seek, or else we wouldn't even be here to live with our misconceptions of space and time, let alone convince ourselves that a can of Campbell's soup painted six feet tall is fine art.

We see actions in time and space as following one another in a linear fashion, this leads to that, cause and effect. What is really happening is that our awareness is jumping from point to point and forming a course that puts the pieces together in our mind from cause (starting point) to effect (end), creating a linear path from moment to moment, hence the illusion of time.

This sounds odd, but if the laws of nature were slightly different, if you jumped on a rock you might turn green and grow an extra set of ears. Most of our rational thought considers the how and not the why. They are not the same. When I fall down and it hurts, it hurts because I scraped my skin and I'm bleeding. We can describe the "who, what, when, where and how" but not the "why". We can explain our physical systems and how pain is created and how it helps us to learn to avoid painful things but we cannot begin to explain why. Asking why is a totally different question and in asking why we will find that the only explanations are found through faith and experience. Why is the sky blue rather than green? We could tell you how it is blue, but not why it is not green. We can all remember being a child and asking, "But why?" over and over because no one had a real answer. Funny thing is that the answer is just "because." Things are simply what they are because that is the way they were meant to be by the One.

Part of our existence is being strung along by these "Just because's" of creation, our splintered awareness being along for the ride. We are born and our awareness attached to a body and we are taken along the course of a man's or woman's life. But we are not just man or woman, not just human. What we truly are is our awareness and this is a little piece of God. Our awareness is blindfolded from the truth so that we may follow through life and feel emotions of pain and happiness, so that we may strive and fail, build and destroy. But really we are not here at all! It is rather funny actually. All of these things that we take to be our own are not ours at all but God's. But this has all been hashed out in earlier of this book.

Now we are in a position to refer back to coincidence. When a coincidence occurs we become partially aware that things are not as they seem. Perhaps we have been thinking of a friend that we miss and the next day they call us out of the blue. What about when a local store that never carries our favorite drink suddenly has it when we stop in on a whim or a gut feeling? The strange feeling we get when our experience confronts our logic during a coincidence can be compared to us going to knock on the door of God to say hello, and then hearing the footsteps coming towards us, freak out and run off before the door can be opened.

There are also instances in our lives called synchronicity. A synchronicity is a coincidence that is far too prevalent for our logical minds to dismiss. In these instances there is an immediacy between two actions that is synchronized in time. This occurs when we are going to pick a phone up to call someone at random and they are already on the line having already called us, or when we have a thought about something which is then immediately verbalized by someone else. Now we are not speaking of when we are at a burger joint thinking of a burger and someone else orders one. This would be something more random such as smoking a cigarette by ourselves and thinking about getting a plaque made of one of our favorite quotes, when another person walking by and talking on a telephone starts talking about plaques with someone else. Now this might be common in a plaque factory, but something like this is very odd anywhere else, especially when synched in time. When a synchronicity occurs we become acutely aware of our relation to existence and it is as if we and God are nodding hello. We are reminded in this moment in an inexplicable way that we are not alone and that we are an inseparable part of a greater existence.

Of course let us not forget deja vu which occurs when we feel that we have been somewhere and done something before. This is because we have! Deja vu is a temporary shift of our awareness from linear to nonlinear time. In this moment we realize that we have done something. It is not that we have done something similar or only dreamed it, it is that we were truly there, in that our greater awareness which is not subject to linear time has experienced it, is still experiencing it. Experiencing deja vu while fully aware is like God patting us on the back and saying, "Good job, buddy, you're on the right path." We should not be freaked out by deja vu, but embrace the experience as an affirmation that we are headed in the right direction.

The next time you experience a coincidence pay close attention. The more aware you become of the little things in life the more likely you are to become aware of the secrets that lie between the cracks of the facade that is our existence. Experience true reality.

Morality

Morality is a tool imposed on man as religious, cultural or governmental law. Morality is not a natural or a universal law. Many moral subjects can coincide with our natural instincts but this is far from a universality which would justify said moralities being imposed as law. If moral issues were universally agreed upon there would be no need for law as a social enforcer. Humans are not built to be a cohesive unit of clones and hence we find ourselves seemingly in need to impose upon others or have imposed upon ourselves a system of controls.

Society forms many controls and uses many systems to implement them. We have a system of courts and police to physically punish those who do not fit in while we also have a system of churches and cultural beliefs that allows groups to mentally force cohesion of their members as well as providing the individual the necessary tools to punish oneself mentally for going against the grain; tools that one may use to mold himself into a model citizen.

The most important aspects of morality are encountered in a culture's morals. It is from we the people that the government is initially given its power to legislate and enforce moral code. It is also we the people that impose our viewpoint over the individual through majority rule, the socialization of youth, mob mentality and violence. These cultural attributes encourage an individual that has been socialized into the system to measure oneself against the social ideal in order to self-correct and avoid possible hostile public or governmental actions.

The tie that binds a culture, whether it is based in religious or political ideals, is inevitably the lowest common denominator. The problem being with this applied theory is that the lowest common denominator is never universal. Take for instance the most prevalent moral of not killing another human being. Most people are naturally inclined to feel disgusted and repulsed by the idea, while a few are completely unaffected by the thought. Making the act of killing illegal serves to stabilize a society against chaos from within while also preserving the meek and fearful from having to defend themselves. With every moral law enacted to solve a problem, more problems are inevitably created.

Now with homicide illegal to anyone but the law, the responsibility for the execution of heinous offenders falls into the hands of the government and serves to isolate people from their government, as in time people will begin to view the government as acting hypocritically. It then becomes an even more confused situation when we the people who have given away our power to rule over ourselves to a government, become sedentary and comfortable in an irresponsible lifestyle. We will then begin to question the government's decisions to enforce a moral code which had originally been placed in their hands by us, but has over time become corrupted and now stands in opposition to our fluid and ever-changing lives. As a lazy and irresponsible people, we begin to embrace idealized and complex morals over those that are simple and pragmatic. So rather than people appreciating the termination of a social danger such as a serial killer we end up having large amounts of people protesting the execution based on moral ground. This is a problem when responsibility, moral or otherwise, is given to the hands of another.

When a government is charged with the stability and security of a society, if the public give up self-responsibility and oversight of the government, or allow for it to become too powerful and take it from them, the public will then begin to degrade into multiple subgroups and countercultures. It is in this that the matters of morality become even more obscured. Historically morality serves as a stabilizer, but when a government grows large and powerful enough to protect its citizens from nearly all threats both external and internal, the public becomes lazy and stops providing oversight over themselves and their government. Eventually we stop caring about the basic necessities of survival because we no longer view them as a threat. When this happens the practice of social stability through the use of morality is soon forgotten. Group consideration in all actions is given up for a mindset of rigid individuality.

    Let us take for example a small farming town. If you drive by a man on the road with a flat tire, you will most likely stop and help him. For one, you know him as your neighbor and it feels good to help. Still yet this kind act will no doubt come back to your favor when you need help, as well as improve the morale of the community when people know that their neighbors are looking out for each other. Now let us consider a large city where you are surrounded by strangers. Here you pass a man on the road with car trouble and keep driving. Why do we do this? To begin with, crime rates are high due to the large population living in relative isolation from each other. We fear that if we should help a stranger we may be robbed, mugged, or even killed. Secondly, there is no emotional bond with the stranger and the individualist's mind will tell us that, "There is nothing in it for me." Without any recompense to name of, we will continue to drive, either completely ignoring the stranded stranger or figuring that someone else will eventually help him. Here the governing system has been given so much control over people's lives that we feel powerless to do anything but look out for ourselves. Why worry about morale or just feeling good helping people, when we could get stabbed helping out and then if we defend ourselves, we could end up being prosecuted?! Why worry about helping the guy out when there are plenty of tow trucks and people willing to help for a buck?

When we en masse give up our power to self-govern and are then oppressed by the system to which we have given up our power, we are most likely going to look out solely for ourselves, as any gathering in numbers over any particular issue is sure to muster the wrath of the government and will be seen as futile. Morals that once were enforced upon the government to take up are now forced upon a people that have no taste or no need for them.

Even as cultures and moralities change from within, the essence of individual self socialization remains the same. Denial, guilt, and feelings of inadequacy are important tools we use on ourselves for this purpose. When we are children we are taught what to do and how to think by our parents and teachers. When we do something that is unacceptable to social expectations we are punished or chastised, likewise when we say something unacceptable. So, early on our opinions and action are shaped through reward and punishment. Eventually we learn how to socialize ourselves by observing what is accepted around us and making ourselves fit the mold. We learn to deny to ourselves any tendencies we may have counter to our culture, and we even go so far as to deny to ourselves that we have such tendencies We learn how to feel inadequate as a means to drive us to be more like everyone else. We learn how to punish ourselves through guilt when we do not add up to our own expectations that have been formed from our culture's expectations. We learn to look to external sources for approval and justification of our feelings, and in doing this we are no longer able to feel genuinely happy being ourselves for we must always seek the approval of others to feel happy. I failed a test, should I feel happy? More likely we will feel bad for failing the test. If we do not feel bad for failing the test, we will soon feel bad for not feeling bad. Either way we will end up not feeling good because we in some way are not a good person by ideal social standards. After this we are plagued by guilt at being a bad person for not fitting in, or being smart enough, or not being good enough or what have you. This guilt will last as long as we feel is necessary to punish ourselves. Then after we feel we have suffered enough to justify ourselves feeling good again, we start to look to others for approval again, either in asking forgiveness for having failed or for new approval on the next test, or game, or job, etc.

It sounds slightly absurd but this is precisely what we do to ourselves until we either notice what we are doing to ourselves and stop ourselves in the act, or become cranky old bastards that just don't care anymore about anything we do. We have so many social beliefs and morals that it is hard to comprehend how many times just today we have acted to socialize ourselves let alone in a lifetime! Sharing, stealing, cheating, bending the rules, punishing, rewarding, producing, working, buying, building, selling, loving, leaving, starting, finishing, failing, excelling, waiting, hurrying, how long do we do this before we can do that, should we feel bad for doing this instead of that, why do we feel good when we do this when we know we should feel bad? With every course of action we are presented with in our lives, our minds are presented with an opportunity to create further socialization or the reinforcement of pre-socialized values.

The question then remains: Once we have admitted to ourselves what we are doing in our own minds, what is morally right and wrong? The only answer to be found is that morality is completely subjective. Here stealing may be wrong, while over there it may be right, just as gravity fluctuates from place to place and time to time so does the rightness or wrongness of an act. We the individual must identify what is morally acceptable, not upon the basis of a social ideal but upon our own judgment of necessity. If you are a starving peasant and you poach food out of necessity, is it really necessary for you to feel any remorse for the act? If you are a businessman, is it right that you should feel nothing but pride for a business transaction that will cost hundreds their jobs and land you a windfall profit? Social morals are not infallible and therefore obedience to them should not go unquestioned.

23.

Trust

Trust is a vague concept but in most of our minds it is a simple black and white idea. The problem that arises from such a mindset is that while we expect people that we trust to act in a particular manner, hardly do others live up to expectations and fit the bill of trust. We constantly find ourselves pulling our trust from others and putting them at a distance from ourselves. So is this then really trust? Can we really trust another person in anything other than varying degrees?

It is quite possible to place full trust in another person but it takes a fluid view of the word trust itself in order to accomplish. We must not conceptualize trust to be anything related to our own imaginings. We speak here again of presumptions.

We are programmed socially to believe that trust in other people can be placed wholeheartedly based upon the innate goodness of humans. The conundrum that we without fail encounter is that people are not innately good, in that no two people share the same conception of what is good, evil, or null.

To illustrate this further, imagine that you loan your car to your buddy so that he may run to the store and buy some beer and junk food. You and your friend have known each other for years and you have been there for each other on multiple occasions and you trust him implicitly, so even though he has never borrowed your car you are not worried in the least. Half an hour later your friend returns and tells you that he has smashed your car into another vehicle on the way back from the store and now your bumper is torn off, and he seems emotionally unaffected.

Now, many of us at this point would immediately begin to question our trust in our friend and vow never to trust them again with anything even of little importance. Many of us would feel hurt, even betrayed at the seemingly callus and unrepentant friend. You can see here that this concept of trust is based on our own delusions and presumptions as to the personality and values of our friend. Rather than accepting that we do not really know even those close to us, we form idealistic constructs of others within our minds. We set ourselves up for disappointment and the dissolution of our trust.

What we should have trust in is not our illusions of people but the actuality of a person. We have a tendency to infer data from past actions and then to presume that it is truthful reality. So when one of our friends is generally trustworthy in this or that action over a period of time we infer from this data that in other activities in the future they will perform in a likewise manner. This is a faulty concept upon which to base trust. You see, there are far too many variables, internal and external, to be calculated that have effect upon another person's psyche. In a section above we have already conversed about the inability for us to truly ever know another, and how especially difficult it can be even to know ourselves. How then do we expect to be able to trust another person based upon presumptive and delusional ideals extracted from faulty and lacking variables? How then do we justify our own anger and contempt when our trust in another has been breached? It is all a little ridiculous.

To move on from here and to trust in the actuality of a person, we must let go of our delusions. In doing this we allow our minds to be free to make real determinations based upon real facts.

What are the facts that are left to us? We do not fully know our friend. We cannot use past data to predict the future actions of our friend, only tendencies We know that values and beliefs are not universal between ourselves and others. We know that we cannot presume to hold others to our own expectations of them. We also know that we should not be angered by others when our illusory preconceptions are shattered nor should we hold these preconceptions in the first place.

What trust then is left to be had? The only trust left to be had is to trust that we can trust no one, or rather that we can trust that we will never know another, nor be able to predict the actions of another. In this is freedom.

When we learn to trust others to be only themselves, we free ourselves of all negative emotions that are attached to our desires of people living up to our own expectations. If someone is a positive influence, we should not have to worry about them betraying our trust and the relationship being destroyed because we now see them as a fluidly changing human and not as a rigid idealized concept. This means that we are never let down, or become sad, angry, distrustful, contemptuous, abandoned, disrespected, the list goes on.

This does not mean that we should surround ourselves with bumbling idiots or shady thieves; it means that our emotional attachment to others, our trust, is bound in action and not illusion. Should someone be a negative force in our life, we should leave them behind just as we would before. If someone is a positive, keep them around. The difference is now in us, not them.

Trust is about freedom and comfortability. If our trust is based in delusion we will suffer much, but if our trust is based upon an understanding of independent thought processes and interdependent interactions we will suffer little. There is little need for negative emotions to be present while plenty of room is left for positive emotion to thrive from our interactions. Again, if someone becomes an inconvenience for our way of life we are at our leisure to move on and away from them. Similarly, now there is no need for us to suffer mentally from others' negative actions as we understand other people are only being themselves and we are simply being ourselves. There is no need to expect from, judge, or mentally suffer anyone.

24.

Self-Doubt

Few things can be as disruptive to ones life as self-doubt. Self-doubt causes us to question our actions and our thoughts. This doubt even goes so far as to corrupt our opinions as to the worth of other people's actions and thoughts. When we speak of self- doubt we are inevitably speaking of self-worth as well.

When we have doubt about our abilities it lowers our self-worth, likewise when we feel we have little worth we begin to doubt our abilities. Like so many other things we encounter, doubt is instilled in us when we are young and do not have the defenses against it. Instead we embrace doubt as necessary and build it into the walls of our mind that shape our world view.

We need to keep in mind that no one fully knows us and what we are capable of. We cannot allow ourselves to be convinced of our abilities simply because we feel dependent upon another's opinion of us for the reinforcement our own self-worth. If we feel that we can reach our dreams, we need only stand up for ourselves and act. Our actions will defeat the negative and empty words we face, and should we fail on our first one or two or ten attempts, we should not crumble to the will of others when we are sure of our own will. Twelve people may tell us that we are wasting our time. Do twelve wrongs make a right? Twelve wrongs can only hope that we never complete our goal so that we may prove them right. We must prove them wrong.

Such things as a parent saying "You can't do that" or a friend saying, "No one from our town will ever get anywhere" discourages us from positive thinking and encourages us instead to be slothful and to discourage others as well. When we develop this sentiment of doubting, whether in order to be cautious so that we may fit in or so that we may never have to fail through trying, the tendency strengthens its grasp over us with each new situation we encounter thus causing the wall it forms in our mind maze to grow thicker and thicker.

Often times we allow outside sources to affect our internal processes simply because we were never taught any different and for many of us it is a natural inclination. Being wholly dependent upon these forces for reinforcement of our beliefs leaves us open to unknown suffering at the hands of others. It is therefore important that we should be able to gather self-worth from within ourselves whilst being independent from and unaffected by external social pressures.

This in itself is no easy solution. On the one hand we all want to feel good about ourselves, while on the other hand we want to fit into our culture and share mutual respect with others. What eventually commences is a balancing act between self identity and social identity. Our individual identity tells us what we like to do, what makes us happy, who we are and the like. Our social identity is what we perceive others perceive in us. He is a good worker, he is polite, he throws good parties, he is a good brother or soldier or citizen, he is educated, he makes really extremely good plain toast.

The conflict arises when our personal self interests butt heads with our social interests. For instance, let' say you really like cheap wine but you are attempting to blend in with a crowd that tend to be wine aficionados. To be yourself you would freely admit that you like cheap wine, but as you are trying to blend in and appease your social self you are likely to compose some wildly ridiculous excuse as to why you cannot name your favorite wine. This is done out of need to have our self-worth approved of by outside sources. This furthers our dependence to external sources just as an addiction grows, and from this, the strength of independent self-worth is marginalized, the social self becoming dominant.

If we instead focus predominantly on the will of the individual mind rather than catering to others we soon find ourselves isolated from them. If we are self absorbed, condescending, or exceedingly eccentric in our ways not only are we isolated from the main of society but we tend to isolate ourselves from other eccentrics in that we will seek ways to prove to ourselves that we are better than them. Selfish thoughts such as, "I am more educated, sophisticated, rogue, nonconformist" and the like provide the necessary ammunition for us to separate ourselves as superior in independence and thus serve to shore up our mental walls of rugged individuality.

The most advisable course of action is to direct our efforts into the cohesion of opposing forces in our mind thus creating a synthesis. We must moderate an agreement between our individual needs and wants versus our social needs and wants. We must draw up a list in our minds, or upon paper should it be easier for us, of these needs and wants. Now we compare the two and observe. If a social need does not affect an individual need then there is nothing to change with it, likewise in opposite. Now, if one need does affect another it is our job to figure out which we value more. We cannot have two opposing desires fulfilled simultaneously.

Which is more important to you, to express your personal opinion and be confident with yourself, or to be accepted into a group and be confident in your social position? In best case scenarios we could both express our opinions, which reinforces our individual self-worth, as well as be accepted by others for being so strong minded, which in turn reinforces our social conception of self-worth, but this is the exception, not the rule.

We must choose what individual aspects of the self we are willing to appease and what aspects of our social self we are willing to appease, as well as what desires and needs we can do without. In ironing out our needs from our desires, both individual and social, we are put in a position to tend our sense of self like a gardener pulling unwanted weeds and sowing needed seeds. When done correctly our sense of self-worth is neither dependent upon external sources nor is it isolated within ourselves as we take the positive influences from both sources while tossing away any negative attributes as useless.

In coming to terms with our interconnectedness with others, and learning to control others' affects over us, we become aware of our self-worth not as some floating concept but as an energetic organism that changes and grows. In seeing this we can begin to understand our Self more readily, and are that much more prepared to achieve full awareness of Self.

25.

To Fight

What is more human than fighting? We have been fighting each other as far back as any man or any document can recall. This is not to say that fighting is inevitable or encouraged but only that we are more apt to raise a call to arms in response to conflicting interests than to open our minds.

We fight to feel powerful and to steal the power of others. We fight for property, materials, and land. We fight out of our hate, lust, envy, greed, sloth, wrath, and pride. Sometimes we fight in defense of love or for survival but far less often than we do for self-serving gains. When we fight out of pride it is for our self, street, city, country, or religion. When for envy, we fight for another's possessions or abilities that we lack and desire. In sloth we fight so that we may have what another possesses so that we do not need to put in our own effort to produce results more easily stolen. When we fight for pride it is to make others cower to reinforce our view of ourselves. When we fight for hate it is because we cannot bring ourselves to understand others in their ways and feel it necessary to crush them simply for existing. In wrath we seek to destroy those that would defy us, while in lust we seek destruction simply for the passion of the act itself.

All of this makes self defense seem so much the more noble option if we are forced to fight. In self defense we fight to protect ourselves from the onslaughts of these attacking forces, we fight to protect those of whom we care about, and our inherent God given rights to life, liberty and the pursuit of happiness.

Fighting then is not something that is completely evil as some would have us believe. Many will tell us that we must be moderating to those that wish to assail us, that we should bend to their wishes so much so that we should remain non-violent even when assaulted with violence. This is an absurdity. All beings have the right to self-defense, and it is our duty to ourselves to retain these rights, by force if necessary. If any party should be required to moderate their opinions it is that of the attacker.

Is it just that a man or group should be forced to give up their property to another group because of the other group's envy or greed? It is not justified and we should not be willing to lose our any of our freedoms in order that an outside party be appeased. A founding father once said to the effect, "They who can give up essential liberty to obtain a little temporary safety deserve neither liberty nor safety. " If we are taught to be unwaveringly non-violent, we are taught to give up whatever rights are demanded of us by another without question! Those of us who would not fight for our liberty will surely have it taken from them, and it will never be restored to any that haven't the strength or force of will to take it back.

What sort of life do we live when we constantly shed our rights? The more that we give in, the more the system is reinforced, the more the system takes. When aggressors are completely unchecked by non-violent non-interventionists an entire population of attackers is created. Now we find ourselves in a dilemma. The only freedom found in a society such as this is found through power plays and in-fighting. Anyone not playing the game is used as a pawn, sacrificed as needed. The pacifists are now stuck in slave wage jobs, toeing the company line, forced to fit into highly rigid social structures in order to just get along. This culture strips us into millions of mindless drones with a handful of kings, and why? Because it is easier to just go along to get along than it is to take an active stake in our own fate.

If we were to take responsibility for ourselves and to act as one force, we would not need to worry about the force put upon us by others within our own system; for the power of rule immediately changes hands when we become aware that it is our power that we have only loaned out to our leaders through laziness, fear, and forgetfulness.

It is wise to concede to an insurmountable force especially if it demands little of us, so that we may live to fight another day. But if an attacking force is conquerable it is our duty to fight it with all our hearts in defense of what is ours, not only for the sake of our rights but also for the sake of preserving our principles.

If we have no principles we have nothing. We are nothing but our actions and the principles that guide our actions. If we concede to accept another's principles by threat of force and not through moderation and communication, we lose control over ourselves and hence we lose ourselves. This is why men of principle would rather die in battle than live as a slave. But as we will no doubt find, it is far easier to find those of us of little principle who are more like cattle, cow-eyed, than it is to find principled humans willing to suffer so that we may retain our dignity. It is saddening to see those cow-eyed people who would trade personal liberty for material security, but it is they who regrettably hold the majority of our numbers.

When considering fighting it is important to note the tendency of men towards cyclical reactionism. When one attacks, another reacts, and then the instigator reacts again. If an attacking force is faced head on with a threatening opponent, the fight may be halted before it begins. If an attacking force feels confident in its ability to overthrow a defending force, any response by the defender will only serve to enrage the attacker and thus, the attacker's reaction will be of growing force with each assault so long as prolonged attack is logistically possible. So a simple fight that may have been avoided if the attacker had been beaten back early on through frightening words or forceful defeat now spins in exponential growth until an apex is met where one side or the other breaks.

Suppose that you are a complete pacifist and you do not support any violent self- protection. Let us also say that your government is taking away the rights of people from free speech to gun ownership to property rights. Perhaps you work to affect change through making large amounts of people aware of what is going on by running an underground newspaper. You hear that presses are being shut down and people arrested and interned for printing anything not authorized by the state. With every paper printed in defiance against the regime, more force is sent out to quell the rebellious acts. With every raid sent out, more equipment and personnel are lost from the rebellion. This of course drives the underground writers to make even bolder statements about the government and therefore the cycle begins again and stronger.

What will you do when you are the next in line? Will you defend yourself against force and stand for your ideals or let your dreams fall to the wayside, praying that another will pick up your principles for you and carry them on? Of what use are you arrested and jailed? What use is your equipment when it is destroyed? If you are assassinated during the raid, what good is even your memory, when people hear that you did nothing to protect yourself, your fellow men or your principles? If others follow your lead they too will bow to conquerors and allow themselves to be taken, peacefully.

Earlier in this collection of writings it was mentioned that violent overthrow of a system will only succeed in breeding a new form of oppression. What is written here is not meant to be hypocritical but rather explanatory of a different situation. In short, it is well that we should fight in our defense from an attacking force, while it is unwise for men to rise up violently and attack an entire system; for to defeat a system, we the people that support that system must be educated of its corruption and given the ability to refute it ourselves. This done, the system crumbles without need of physical force. To do otherwise results in the division of men as we are forced choose between that which we have grown accustomed to through education and media, and that which a group of violent men whom our system brands as traitors call freedom. Which choice comes more naturally?

So you see, for a few to fight with a system is futile, while if we the people in mass who make up the system are brought to question our support, then the system changes. A few may have effect but only in that their actions may guide the minds of others. If it is the goal of the few to guide other minds in a nonviolent fashion towards a brighter mutual future, it is then unjustified that a system should crush a rebellion solely out of survival instinct. In this case, should peacefully rebelling men come under attack through violence and/or incarceration it is their justified right and duty to defend themselves, their ideals, and their comrades through equal or elevated use of force.

As for a system attacked from outside, it is the right and duty of the system that has been granted the power over itself from we the people, to deny any external power from interfering with its abilities to retain life, liberty, and the pursuit of happiness.

We must defend our principles in mind, in speech, and in action. We cannot seek to impose our views upon others by force. We must not be drawn into a fight that we cannot win. When we are forced to fight, we must fight to win. When an aggressor first moves against us, that aggressor gives up its neutral status and is therefore subject to annihilation due to its violation of another's liberty. We must not be fooled into comparing our treatment of an enemy with our treatment of a friend or neutral party. To truly win we must completely destroy our enemy's ability to fight. This may mean to discredit in media, to battle in court, kill in self-defense, or to devastate an entire population in war. To fight with anything less than the full force necessary to affect a resounding victory is to welcome our own defeat. Victory is not temporary restraint of our enemy, but total domination.

26.

Free Thinking

Consciousness is a gift to some, a curse to others. How nice it would be simply to live as we fancy animals do, with no concept of time, no guilt, no understanding of science. If only we could un-know everything we do know and live in harmony subject to the whims of nature. But alas, we are subject instead to minds that comprehend and categorize the world around us. We are forced by our own natures, by the observations and analysis of cause and effect, to suffer our foreknowledge of the future. The nature of our minds controls our actions and drives us to desire control over everything in our lives that we may conceivably force to bend to our wills.

Under each of our facades, sometimes deep within, sometimes closer to the surface, we all understand that we are bound to certain unchangeable traits, traits that are innate to our being, perhaps bound by genetics, the soul, or both. Among these traits is our natural inclination to seek control. How deeply buried in our consciousness this recognition of our nature is located is directly correlated with our ability or lack thereof to think freely.

You see, the more likely we are to bury away a truth from ourselves, the more likely we are to actively work to blind ourselves from any information contradictory from the world view that we already have in mind. In this, free thinking becomes less and less free the more we act to hinder our own mind's interaction with external sources. For free thinking is to think unconstrained by preconceptions. To think freely is to attack with ferocity the preconceptions and assumptions of others. If we are already so afraid of our own selves that we would not investigate into our own hearts and minds, it would be ridiculous to attempt delve into those of others. Not only would the attempt be ridiculous, but it would be futile. What information can we glean from another, when all incoming information is filtered through our own preconceptions and a maze of mental walls set up to block input harmful to a rigid world view? This is why there is a direct correlation between our willingness to recognize our own nature and our ability to think freely.

To think freely we must let go of all that we hold sacred that makes up our own conception of self. What do you think of politics, society, humanity, art, science, religion, human rights, civic duty, food, animals, agriculture, Play-Doh or Playboy? It doesn't matter. Free thinking is not about the festering of our own stifled thoughts commingling but is rather about the free interaction of our mind with raw information, unattached to any of our own preconceptions.

In freethinking we let our mind move at its own speed and in its own direction. We do not attempt to direct the flow of information or control its speed of calculation. Information is considered not through a filter of our own convenient design, but as the raw data that it is. In treating information as raw and unbiased we do not attempt to color it this way or that, nor do we attempt to make the information fit where we think it should. This is the main problem that arises when confronting new information.

Let us say for example that you are a city slicker and you go out west on a business trip. You are in a small town at a bar after a meeting and you strike up a conversation with a local. The local proceeds to tell you all about the small town and how wonderful it is to live there. At this point your preconceived biases come into play. You may assume that all small town inhabitants are ill-educated. You may assume that they are not well traveled and don't know how great your own city is. You may assume from this local's clothing, whether dirty or old, his social status. You may even assume his mental capabilities depending on his usage of language. Now this is but a short list of ways in which one may allow their preconceptions to shade information. Imagine what else goes unlisted. Imagine what else we may do to dilute raw information into tainted reinforcement of our own rigid mindsets?!

  What we should do instead while conversing with the man in the bar, or while observing the social customs of a pack of wild snails, is to first empty ourselves of all expectations. Then, throw all suppositions, assumptions, preconceptions, and any other "tions" that are in the way. We must empty our minds of all thought and allow the purest information possible to flow into an accepting mind. Don't see the spider as ugly when compared to a puppy. See the spider as it is. See the beauty of its form built so well for its function. See how wonderfully it affects your base emotions. See how it builds its trap and how skilled a hunter it is.

  When we encounter something that we have built up so many walls around in our mind, the first thing we do is throw up those walls against it. With these walls already in place, it is more likely that even more will form as in a crystalline structure, like a tiny particle of ice growing into snowflake. What do we see when we encounter something we already fear? The spider remains terrifying and when we attempt to ignore it, we allow more walls to grow within us until this fearful object becomes an immovable mountain in our mind. Hence when we come into contact with these monsters in our everyday life we either immediately block them out of our consciousness or we react in a violent fashion when our fight or flight survival instincts kick into gear. As you can see it would be rather hard to observe the cultural changes implicated in an economic reorienting of a nation's infrastructure or the mating habits of collegiate students on a Thursday night, when mentally we are busy running around and screaming as if we were on fire.

    To think freely we must take nothing to heart save truth. We must question the world view of society as well as our own. We must not take opinions as fact while we compare commonly accepted knowledge to real world events. We must explore all the possibilities that lie within our minds and in the wide expanses of existence while clinging to none. Our minds must be free from attachment if we are to truly embrace freethinking.

27.

Mindfulness

Mindfulness is the art of directing thought. It is also the art of directing non-thought. It is very important throughout our daily lives that we should be able to think thoughts so that we may be able to balance our bank accounts or take the right exit off of the highway. Or was I supposed to go left?

Mindfulness is concentration, but not only upon running calculating thoughts through our head, but in ensuring that we are not letting our heads get carried away with themselves. To maintain this concentration it is important first that we learn to let go. We must let go of our desires when they are haunting us. We must let go of problems which we cannot in the time being solve. We must let go of worry!

How do we do this? This is done by admitting to ourselves that we are not perfect and that we don't need to be. We need to realize and come to terms with the idea that we have no control. If we let go of our obsession with control and the systematic compartmentalization of input and output of information, we can allow our minds a chance to breathe.

The obsession of "thinking" all the time is quite dangerous. If we are constantly thinking rather than experiencing, life just passes us by without any real enjoyment. When we are driving and we miss our exit, is for a lack of mindfulness. We are dangerously out of focus here as thoughts of the day behind us go racing through our head and we are caught thinking about everything in life outside of where and what we are currently doing.

On the other hand, if we have no thought or reason in our head, we may very likely drive just as dangerously. Mindfulness is the balance of thought and experience.

28.

Thought

Do not think too much. Too much consideration breeds inactivity. Then again, too much action without thought is dangerous. Our minds can run wild with thoughts, at times keeping us more occupied with possibilities of the future or of past events. When we allow our minds to dysfunction in such a manner it pulls us out of the present moment. There is no moment but the present and we must remain persistent in our seeking to remain fully conscious right here and right now. It would be ill-advised not to learn from the past or to prepare for the future but we should not become fixated with one or the other. It is important to gather what we can from our past and move on, and likewise to allow ourselves to relax in the acceptance that we cannot control the future.

We should not try to force thought. When we force our thoughts it degrades what we produce from them. For example, a play that is written from someone's personal experience and natural imagination is far more pleasing than a sitcom episode that is written out of regurgitated scripts and a forced timeline. What we produce from our thoughts is more pleasing if it is produced naturally versus unnaturally forced. This is likened to comparing an original Van Gogh and a machine-made reproduction or worse yet, a spin off painting done in the same style by an imitator.

There is a flow to thought that if ignored produces inharmonious and generic actions; but if recognized and embraced, brings about beautiful and organic manifestations. The natural flow of our mind is organic of itself and so is accustomed to peaks and troughs of activity. The flow of creative thought is different from person to person and time from time but with practice we are able to harness our thoughts more often and can learn how to encourage a waning thought flow into a waxing state.

So, rather than attempting to force an incoherent idea with a sense of immediacy, we who are well versed in the navigating and tending of our own minds are able to guide and direct our thought flow in the desired direction. This allows us to meet time-lines without the strain and stress that go with forced thoughts as well as providing creative rather than bland productions.

Thought control is the very art by which we control our minds and our actions. When we change something we do not like about ourselves or something in the outside world it is through our thoughts that we do these things. It is of dire importance than that we should learn to control our thoughts, in that with controlling our thoughts we can control our experience of existence.

Let us not confuse our terminology. Here, when we say control of thoughts we are not speaking as if we want to control in the same fashion that we would harness and tame a wild animal. What we mean by control is to guide and direct our thoughts by means of our will as we would if we were to divert water in a creek. The raw energy of the flow is still left intact while the end goal is still attained. If we instead try and force our thought, using force of will against the natural force of our thought, something is going to break and the end result is not going to be pretty, and our intended goal will remain unaccomplished.

29.

Experience

30.

Money

The problem with money is that we often confuse money with happiness. We use money when we buy clothes, food, and other necessities but we also use money to open up doors of opportunistic experience. This latter usage of money is where the confusion seeps into our consciousness.

It is fun to do different things and live through a variety of experiences. With money we can go pay for a boat to go boating or afford to take a friend out to dinner. It is not the money that makes us happy but our interactions with our surroundings and other people. When we become dependent upon certain circumstances in order to let ourselves feel happy then the confusion of equating money with happiness begins to control us.

Let us say that you have a boat and you and your friends go out on the lake every weekend in the summer and drink and go tubing and eat at dockside restaurants around the lake. Now if we are an adaptable person, if we do not have the money at some point to fund these outings we will simply find something else to make us happy that we can afford to do. Others though are not so adaptable and so may find themselves working extra hours and extra jobs in order to afford happiness once a week. In this case people "trade in their hours for a handful of dimes", living not in the moment and striving to be contented, but rather we eternally suffer, living in a dream of the future. This cheapens not only us but our relationships and our future experiences with our friends and family, as now we begin to see life not as interactions to experience but THINGS to attain. This is called grasping and is unhealthy.

Trying to hold on to things, grasping, is at root simply an error in terminology. If we consider our world as made up of static things, rather than its more truthful state of being constructed of transitory interactions, we are doing ourselves a grave disservice. When we attempt to grasp it is because we think that we can hold on to a thing, when in fact what we are doing is attempting to grasp an interaction. This is like trying to grab hold of the wind. Something that happened in the past that we want again, or something that we have never had and want in the future can become conceptualized in our minds as static things. This is a tendency that is formed in our head throughout our lives but it is not natural in the strict sense that it is not an aspect of our minds that we are born with and must carry on till death. At any time we are free to shed our misconceived notions of nature being made of static things that remain unchanged over time and that can be grasped.

The negative aspects of money are very much related to our tendencies to live in memories or fantasies of the future. Focusing on the gathering of money allows us to fool ourselves into believing that we have control in our life. The more money we have the more able we are to do things on our own terms. But, what we do not see is that this money is controlling and directing us like a carrot on a stick leading a donkey.

The more we allow ourselves to fall under the spell of power, the less we are ourselves, in that this power we seek ends up turning us into its slave. It is very much like an addiction. I see that this much money allows me to drive my motorcycle once a month on a road trip. I wonder how much money I would need to do it every weekend? When we set our eyes on desires that are beyond our means we can do one of two things: we can either adapt our minds to get along without them, or adjust our actions in order to grab them.

The problem with adjusting our lives to grasp things is that once we do it for something we desire, is easier the next time to trade in our immediate happiness for an imaginary future happiness. Eventually we may find ourselves working and working at something that makes us miserable in order so that in some far off and possibly non- existent future we may be happy. This is not to say that we should not work for what we desire but that we should not offer up our true happiness, which is to be content and aware of the ever present moment, for future happiness that is ephemeral or even non-existent. This is the danger of forming a fixation upon money.

Drugs

Such a stigma has been attached to drugs that it is difficult for many people to even speak of them without some emotional upsurge. The problems that we face with drug use on a personal and societal level are not simply a matter of the drugs themselves but the manner in which they are misused and abused.

Much of our opinion is shaped today by media representations. What we tend to forget is that in the media, whether in cinema, television programs, or the news, subject matter is routinely blown out of proportion for the sake of shock effect, in order to grab the attention of an audience. When we forget the nature of the media and allow ourselves to be convinced of its half truths, we generally fall into step with their presentations and then end up perpetuating these false perceptions within our own communities. What started as political propaganda nearly a century ago in the United States has now become popular opinion and is accepted in large part as fact.

Stereotypes represent illegal drug users as stupid, lazy, violent, criminal, unclean, irresponsible, dangerous, psychotic, and delusional. It is wildly hypocritical of a society to preach understanding and tolerance and the banishing of stereotypes, and then turn around and reinforce other stereotypes. Though some of these attributes may describe some illegal drug users, they may also be used to describe hundreds of other groups. Let us consider soccer moms that pop prescriptions pills like candy, doctors that abuse alcohol and all of us that use tobacco and caffeine.

Illegal drugs have had a taboo placed upon them in the consciousness of our society while legal drugs are considered fine for abuse and in many cases are not even considered drugs. What we will find when comparing groups of people that use illegal drugs, those that use legal drugs, as well as those of us that use none at all, is that there are trends popular to each group; but the stereotypes attributed to illegal drug users can be found in members of each of these groups as a matter of an individual's nature not necessarily stemming from one's use or lack of use of drugs.

Criminal activity can be found in a health-conscious non-drug user just as much in one that uses licit or illicit drugs. Violent and dangerous behavior for instance can be found in bountiful numbers in communities around the world that strictly forbid all kinds of drugs. Ever been to the Middle East? As for stupid people, it doesn't matter where in the world we find ourselves, drugs or not, there will be plenty of stupid people doing stupid things.

Much of the animosity towards illegal drug users is perpetuated by those of us that relate our sense of self to our society. People who, as in the United States, value consumerism, productivity, and the sacrificing of personal freedom for monetary gain tend to become angered when confronted with another that does not hold their same values. By coming into contact with such a person, those of us that are focused on fitting in become defensive because if someone else questions our social ideals, they are in effect questioning the value of our own self. This accounts for some of the hypocrisy related to the popular opinion about drug users. Those of us who that take the party line and judge ourselves by the eye of society are extremely willing to toe the party line when given the chance elevate ourselves by identifying another human as repugnant.

The reasons for the illegality of certain drugs is not so much that they are always more dangerous than legal drugs but that they threaten the social system. Ours is a dominant and centralized system that controls not only our movement, but through education and media, our thoughts. When our society's ideals of life, liberty, and the pursuit of happiness have become replaced with those of corporatism, consumerism, mindless follower-ship etc, it is necessary for the continuation of this corrupted society that it re-educate, enforce upon itself, and perpetuate these corrupt values.

For the most part, public education and media promote perceptions sufficient to control the minds of the public into a herd of mindless, lock-stepping, Nazi-esque, cow-eyed worker drones. There are though certain things that have the ability to shock us out of our waking slumber. Sudden death experiences, seeing the face of war, the raising of a child etc; these instances have the capability to open the mind, but do not have an excellent success rate. Drugs can also open the mind and with a far superior rate of return, but drugs being a material substance can be controlled.

The difference between legal drugs and illegal drugs is in their ability to either make us easier to control or more independent. Legal drugs such as alcohol and nicotine depress the body and mind and thus users of them can self-medicate to cope with stress, or rather mask symptoms while ignoring the actual stressors. Legal uppers such as caffeine and taurine give an energy boost to the body while having little effect on the mind save to make us jumpy. Illegal drugs such as marijuana, LSD, heroine, opium, hash, mescaline, and mushrooms, have varying levels of psychotropic effects. In short these drugs allow us to experience things in a way that illuminates the inner working of our own minds. This type of experience immediately calls the world view of the drug user into question, and opens up a window of opportunity for us to explore our conceptions of the world that have been taken for granted since birth. This is what societies and governments find threatening about these drugs. If we are no longer attached to a society for our sense of self then it is possible for us to act in a way that is harmful to the stability of society.

This calls into question the state of a society itself when it is more concerned about its own survival than with the individual mental and spiritual enlightenment of its citizens. It is the duty of a society to fit the needs of its people, not the duty of a government to force the people to fit into a society. But in the times in which we live our government no longer requires the mandate of the people but rather forces its mandate upon us.

With the use of psychoactive drugs to give ourselves a glimpse of something outside of our normal range of view, there comes not only the danger of persecution from government and the brainwashed citizenry, but the dangers of dependent addiction. Dependency as we spoke of earlier can be formed for many reasons; with drugs though it is largely out of sloth.

When we are addicted out of sloth it is that we find it easier to mask the symptoms of our personal problems with drugs use than to actually fix our problems. This is not relegated solely to illegal drugs but is quite prevalent in persons that use alcohol and prescription drugs as well. Why should I look into myself and my problems when instead I can place the blame elsewhere and drink away my pain? Why should I confront my issues which I am ashamed of, when I can kill my feelings with drugs prescribed by a physician? This kind of drug abuse will generally continue in a downward spiral until we are either out of money, dead, publicly embarrassed, or worse. Sometimes the spiral doesn't end with those of us who have the sheer stubbornness to keep at it, no matter what ill befalls us, ending in the gutter.

There is another kind of drug abuse that is not as dangerous as using drugs as an escape from troubles, but can be wasteful in its nature and potentially deadly in its recklessness. Recreational drug use is the most popular form of drug use and involves all types of drugs from the legal to the illegal. The most dangerous aspect of using drugs for fun is that we can become comfortable with the casual usages of multiple forms of drugs and thus can become careless when using these substances. Rather then doing just enough to mask our issues such as those mentioned above, recreational users search for the next best thing. Sometimes this involves using higher doses, while other times it involves trying different substances or mixing multiple kinds at once. It is in becoming comfortable in casually upping doses or mixing and matching that can cause overdosing and physical addiction.

Aside from the physical effects of recreational use, there is also a mental and spiritual side effect that can occur when toying with drugs. In using psychoactive drugs, if we are not mindful of their properties we may be overwhelmed by them. Certain people have minds that are extremely unaffected by experience whereas some of our minds are extremely vulnerable. Those that are strong in will are less likely to be affected negatively by psychotropics while those of us with weak wills are far more apt to break.

Psychotropics can suddenly cause the walls of perception in our minds to crumble. If we have a rigid mindset and a weak will there is a distinct possibility of us going quite mad. If we have a fluid mindset but weak will, we will be highly influenced by our experiences under the drug but not know what to properly make of them, perhaps developing new issues or being thrown into a contemplative stupor for months or years. Those of us with rigid or fluid perceptions but strong wills will come out safe. The rigid and strong willed will learn nothing of their experience, but misuse drugs for the sake of entertainment. Those who are fluid-minded and strong-willed will learn from their experiences and use drugs for the sake of research.

Sex, Sin, and Self

We are constantly confronted by contradictory information regarding sexuality and it can be hard to draw our own opinions on the subject. While the media portrays gratuitous scenes of overt sexuality, our social institutions purport to abhor public displays of affection or any action behind closed doors that does not fit in with a fanatical idealism.

Sex need not be a taboo subject, yet it is so often an uncomfortable subject. Why is it that we can talk about a physical act of sex with our friends and not our parents without it becoming uncomfortable? Why is it that we can watch a program on television that is showing group sex or swapping of partners and become fascinated, while we are disgusted or pass judgment on any of our friends we find out have engaged in similar acts?

Somewhere in our minds when we are growing up is implanted the idea that sexuality is unclean. Then as we grow older and develop desires, we then act upon them and decide that sexual acts are not bad after all, yet when in social situations we still convey to others and ourselves that we still consider sex as morally wrong somehow.

In the United States we have been influenced by puritanical forces from the pilgrims, to the religious right of the Bible belt today. The moral problems with sex arise from religious interpretations that believe that the human body, and for that matter the material world in itself, is full of evil. This is a misinterpretation of the nature of existence. The moral conservatives would have us believe that the world is evil and that salvation exists only after we have left this cursed flesh. The aim of the puritanical is to live without falling into corruptions through temptations of the flesh. This is in itself is a poor phrase, for to state "temptations of the flesh" will lead some of us to believe that our flesh itself is evil, while what it actually refers to are worldly temptations. This though is exactly where extremists gather their support. People that are not gifted with an intellect that can read between the lines or think for itself, take the word of God as literal, or worse, the word of their preacher/imam/priest as THE WORD. When people literally believe that our flesh is evil, the idea of sexual interaction with another sounds doubly evil.

Though zealots may have a basic understanding of the evil of the material world they misunderstand our relationship with this world. In their view we are to avoid all evils in order that we may go to heaven after we die. This makes the assumption that our ego is retained after death. It also falsely assumes that this ego of ours is going to live in a heavenly paradise if we avoid these evils. Lastly this idea assumes that there is no way to avoid being corrupted by evil in this world other than by avoiding as much contact as possible with worldly things.

Our society's problem with sexuality is then not rooted in the evil of flesh but in the intellectual and spiritual ineptitude of the weak-willed. We have already discussed the self at length and we know better than to buy into the idea of an eternal ego. Let us cover the topic of heaven then. If there is a heaven after death it is enjoyed by the soul not the ego. This heaven after death would not be a place of egocentric paradise but a state of being with a closer and less enigmatic relationship with the Godhead. The heaven that does exist for the ego lies here on earth. The only heaven a human ego will ever experience will be entered when we have fully understood the Self and experienced the relationship of our self to God, which effectively obliterates our concept of independent self. This said, the presumption of getting to heaven by avoiding the pleasure of the flesh still stands.

Some may take what is written above and assume that perhaps we should attain heaven by understanding the Self via puritanical shirking of worldly sins such as sex. We must then pose this question: How do we understand the Self when we are constantly avoiding interactions which would help lead us to understand our Self? To do this would assume that we already know our Self and what it needs, or even that someone else is better to guide us than ourselves, i.e. a church group or preacher.

The Self is formed by the interactions of mind, body, and soul and the outside world. If we are not free to observe how the Self is formed (because we are living a sheltered and controlled life) then how are we to learn to deconstruct it and understand it? If we are puritanical, how are we to understand the Self when the material world is evil and the Self which we identify as ourselves is in part material? Surely we would shy away from understanding the Self, for if we would understand this we would recognize that by our own belief system this makes our own Self evil.

Ultimately there is no arguing with a fundamentalist; inevitably the answers we will receive when we have exhausted a line of questioning will be "because". If a line of text taken literally cannot back them up then there will be a sudden appearance of magical ability on the part of their God to do something not even covered in the their literal text.

The taboo of sex is heavily based in the mindsets of these small-minded creatures, who are determined to control the lives of the rest of us out of the fear of their own inadequacies and inabilities to control their own will. It all comes back to personal responsibility, and those that lack the ability or fortitude to be responsible for themselves try to force homogenization upon others in order to reinforce their own ill-founded world views.

Experiencing the world around us and developing our Self in order to shape our souls is the entire reason we exist as we do. If we deny the world and worldly things completely we would die! We are of this world and there is no way around it. Human beings need interactions with other humans as much as we need food and water. Included in the realms of human interaction is sexual interaction. Is it not hypocritical to admit our dependency on food and water, spend years working and acquiring material wealth and then deny that we should openly enjoy worldly things? This is like a fish saying, "I need water to live but I am going to swim and explore as little as possible because it is wrong to be a fish, and I shouldn't enjoy it when I should be with God instead, so I'm just going to bide my time until then and try to be as un-fishlike as possible." If I were a fish I should like to think I would be as fishy as possible and do all things a fish could do.

We humans get a bit carried away with our minds sometimes to the extent that we shun the world outside of it. This is all well and good if we would like to waste our lives acting like fish that do not want to be fish. Like it or not we are human and the world we live in is full of potential human experiences. It is our duty as created beings to act in the full spectrum of human behavior. This in itself justifies any mindset we choose, including Puritanism; but finds all other mindsets as equally valid. Should we prefer a mindset that is based in experience, logic, adaptability, love and understanding or one that is based on idealistic myth, hate, fear, judgmentalism, and rigidity?

The realm of sexual interaction is wide open to those of us with a mindset of openness. With nothing to fear from experiences that may contradict our beliefs, since none do, we are free to explore sexuality without damaging our sense of Self. The only factors that limit "sinful" interactions are one's own perceptions. Fear of being seen with someone, fear of being judged, fear of turning into a deviant, fear of knowing ourselves: irrational fears, but which stem from our mindset being focused upon social expectations rather than our own personal experiential exploration. The only worries we should concern ourselves with is whether or not we use protection and if another person has sexually transmitted diseases. This is not to say that we should run around having sex with everyone we run into at the expense of other people, but that we should be free to act as we desire sexually, in a responsible libertarian manner.

33.
Guilt

Remorse is unjustified when we are assuredly not in the wrong. No one may judge our guiltiness save we ourselves, furthermore the choices we make are not solely ours and are influenced and set into action by the force of events preceding our current moment in time and tracing back to the birth of existence itself.

In every moment we are at our best. Even when we stoop to our lowest or lose control of ourselves, when we are at our worst, we are still doing the best that we can at that moment. It is not ridiculous that we should feel guilt or remorse over our past actions when we do not control who we are, but that we are simply egos formed by our existential conditions?

As referred to earlier in this book, you are not you; you are God, though you seem to be suffering a little self-imposed amnesia. That is truly what the egocentric Self is: amnesia, the experience of separateness from God. Although we experience this separateness, it is not the full truth. There is no separateness from God, only the illusion of this division. As such, not only is all that we are an ego predetermined by the evolution of existence, but as being part of this existence created of God, whatever it is that we do happens within God. Now if The Source created a universe, knows everything about that existence, and continues to let it run its own course, should we really feel guilty about being late for a lunch date, or forgetting an anniversary?

Everything that is happening has happened before and will happen again.

Slight variations of course may occur, but the basic principles that create existence and the Self, time and space, everything that composes this duality, constantly repeat in the fashion of a fractal, never ending, never starting. This being the case, why should we feel guilty about missing a car payment or not being completely honest in confession?

The problem with guilt then lies in our conception of the Self. To truly rid ourselves of the negative effects of guilt we must rid ourselves of our false conceptions of Self. We must admit that though we do exist after a fashion, we are not independent of the world or of God. We must dis-attach ourselves from this view that the Self can be fashioned by our own hand and that our futures are shaped by free will. There is no free will in the sense that we command our own destinies. How could we command our own destinies if we are so interwoven with the fabric of nature, that not only do we have no separate Self of which to command, we have no objectivity with which to guide our will freely?

We must let go of the ego, it is not ours to hold and is an ephemeral illusion. Our true Self is held by God. We need to let go of our guilt, the actions and decisions we have made in the past were the only actions and decisions possible for us to make. Our actions are initiated by God. The "who, what, when, where, why", and how that defines us is not our decision to make. The only decisions we are allowed to make are simply for show. We are not the puppeteer of our minds and bodies, we are the puppets. Why should we, the puppet, feel any remorse for the actions done through us by a puppeteer?! It is ridiculous to suffer simply for the sake of our own vanity and denial. Stop denying the true nature of the Self from yourself! There, no more guilt.

Happiness

Odd as it may sound, it is actually a bad idea to seek happiness. Because happiness is one part of a dualistic continuum, happiness-sadness, the more we seek happiness the more we find sadness. The more able we are to feel happy the more deeply we feel sorrow. It is not that happiness is a bad thing in itself, it is after all the feeling of being happy, but the chasing of happiness serves to perpetuate sadness. This perpetuation of sadness occurs because of our grasping desire for happiness. It is through desire that our awareness is pulled out of unity with the ground of all being and into the world of dual conditions.

Desires are what cause suffering. When we are not content it is because we are not comfortable in our own skin; we are not comfortable in the here and now. This discomfort generally leads to the growth of desires within us for a different here and now, a different situation. When we allow ourselves to become sad, we desire happiness. When we are uncomfortable being happy, as when we see others being sad (perhaps at a funeral), we desire that we should be sad as well so as to relate, and if we do not immediately feel sadness then we encourage guilt to form in order to encourage our sadness.

Clearly happiness is a wonderful feeling to enjoy and most of us would prefer to feel happiness a much as possible. What we must not do though is to crave happiness. The ups and downs of life come at us like the peaks and troughs of waves. Life is a constantly changing and dualistic environment; we cannot expect that we will always be happy. What we can do though is control the affect on our minds that external influences have.

Much like Pavlov trained his dogs to manifest responses to stimuli, we too can train ourselves to control our responses. Through self-study and mental discipline we can reprogram our socialized tendencies to better suit our personal needs. To do this we must learn not only how and what we react to, but also how to control our reactions, our emotional responses.

For the sake of argument let us assume that you get hired at a cheese factory. You have hated the smell of cheese for as many years as you can remember, in fact it makes you slightly homicidal. Sadly, all the jobs as international spies and beer pong tournament judges in your town are filled so you are forced to work where you can. Now, if you are going to work at this place for any extended time without causing significant harm to yourself or others you are going to need to reprogram your response to cheese. We know how you react, violently. We know what you react to, that god-awful cheese that's been looking at you funny. What we need to find out next is how to control your response to this wicked piece of curdled milk.

The first step in controlling our responses is to understand where in our mind they are coming from. It is wrong to assume that our responses are coming from an external influence. External influences only trigger pre-programmed responses that we have taught ourselves through socialization and habit. So, we must figure out where in our mind these pre-programmed responses are coming from. Simply put, they are coming from associated memories. These memories can be buried deep in our minds because they are unneeded; after we have associated these memories on a few occasions to fashion a response, our mind goes into automatic, thus forming habitual responses for future use.

The response of becoming angry when smelling cheese may be related to an early childhood memory of eating cheese and maybe throwing up and then being laughed at which made you angry. Perhaps a bully smeared cheese all over your face and you were too weak to fight back and that made you angry. Honestly, there are millions of possible combinations of past events that can form a trigger and a response in our minds. It is up to each of us ourselves to dig them out of that muck up there in our heads.

After our triggers and the memories associated with them are understood we can go about fixing our responses. The fixing begins when we attack the problem at the root. The root of our problem is not the cheese, or our response, but it is our fixation upon a past event that we for some reason cannot come to terms with. What was the traumatic event for you and what aspect of it haunts you? Is it a matter of pride, lack of control, fear, self-pity, etc? When we discover the issue at hand and take the time to come to terms with it; when we actually deal with our issues, they dissolve.

By dissolving our issues we dissolve the main elements of a triggered response but we of course still have a ghost left behind. Although we have destroyed the foundation and reinforcement of a triggered response we still have the habit to break. Now that our issues have been dealt with, the habitual response has no foundation or reinforcement for future function, unless we feed the animal. If we continue to nurture our habitual responses by allowing them to proceed indefinitely and automatically, then they will. This is just the way our minds our built. But if we consciously intervene when a habitual response is popping up its ugly head, then it will soon die off of its own accord.

Habitual responses are like an adaptive AI in a computer. They are designed to allow for faster performance with less computation. When the AI sees that its responses are no longer allowing the mind and body of a person to function faster and easier, but rather hindering the person's performance, then the AI rewrites its program and automates a different set of routines.

The way that we intervene with habitual responses is to first halt the actions that they direct us to do, and then implant a desired trigger and response. You smell the cheese, it no longer makes you angry, you fight the urge to smash someone's face in; then you tell yourself that cheese is good. In your mind you now must visualize new memory imprints to emplace as the new trigger. Picture yourself walking down the beach holding hands with a block of cheese, sun shining, waves crashing, and money raining from the sky. While you do this, you breathe in the smell of the cheese.

Visualize good things; associate them with the external influence. From here we can program our response: perhaps you will smile when smelling cheese, perhaps you will feel secure, or maybe you would prefer to imagine making sweet love to a life-sized piece of cheese dressed up like a floozy while cruising around the solar system on an asteroid made of frozen unicorn teardrops.

The problem many of us have when approaching this method of self-control is that we often can feel that it is inhuman for us to control ourselves as if we were a machine that can have its operating code edited. This indeed sounds very cold.

We should remember though that when we are babies and children first learning how to act, when we are socialized, what we are doing is hard-wiring our responses to external information. As we grow older we continue to form our internal network, though we do so more based upon our unconscious and previous constructions than upon our conscious will.

It is after all completely human of us to program ourselves. It is the pain of admitting to ourselves that we are organic machines and not a supernatural phenomenon that prevents us from reprogramming ourselves according to our own wills. This goes back to the idea of independent Self being based upon a social ideal.

If we relate to a society that believes emotional roller coasters and uncontrollable reactions are what make us human, then we as socialized members of that society feel that if we control our emotions and do not suffer roller coasters that we are inhuman. Popular belief is not necessarily truth but can often be instead socially reinforced misconceptions. If we, rather than identify our Self with our social ideals, identify our Self based upon our own contemplations and observations, we will find that it is more than acceptable to take responsibility for the condition of our mind and the actions that we manifest through it.

It is quite ironic actually that the more we act as if we are independent of nature the more we are controlled by our emotions and mental constructions as if we were mindless machines, while the more we accept our true nature of interdependence, the less we are controlled, the less automated we act, and the much more vibrant we actually become!

When we seek happiness it is because of our inability to control ourselves and remain content in any given situation. When we can control the actions of our minds we control the entire perceived world around us. What today is an ugly landscape of desolation, fear, anxiety, and sadness, tomorrow can be as beautiful and peaceful as anything you can imagine. Trying to escape pain and suffering by grasping and craving for a light in the dark only perpetuates our ordeals.

Living for this evening's beer, next year's promotion, this weekend's visit with the lover, all this will only serve to mask the symptoms of our suffering for an ephemeral ecstasy, just so that we may begin drowning again. Rather than looking for this flickering light in the dark, if we look into ourselves, we will find that the light is on everywhere; we just have forgotten to turn up the dimmer switch.

There is no perpetual happiness to be had on this earth for reasons already explained. The nearest state with which to find is contentedness. To be content does not mean that we do not laugh or smile or act cheerfully at times. To be content is to remain in a constant state of emotional balance, never letting ourselves become engulfed in the anguish of negative emotions and get carried away. To be content is to enjoy positive emotions such as happiness and love but with much attention as to avoid the formation of attachment, as we know attachments breed desire, craving, and suffering. To be content is to let life come at us as it will and remain internally stable, outwardly calm as our mind fluidly and consciously reacts to external influences. To be content is to appreciate the good, the bad, and the ugly while attaching ourselves to nothing. To be content is to feel the full range of human emotion but to control and direct our own emotions while understanding empathetically those of others. To be content is to never be cold or distant from reality or from those with which we interact, but to be fully aware and involved in life while maintaining the steady source of our contentedness.

35.
Leadership

More often then not we will find our leaders lacking in leadership. This is not so much a result of personal inabilities as it is of culturally acceptable corruption and irresponsibility. What we find is that the majority of people that are put into positions of leadership are seeking to gather power for personal reasons rather then seeking to utilize the power bestowed upon them in order to serve those they lead.

Corrupted and irresponsible leadership is widespread and immensely destructive to business, religion, people, militaries, families etc. Our nature determines that we organize ourselves in hierarchical structures, and from the smallest groups to the largest international organizations, we control ourselves with these structures. It is of grave importance then that those who lead us do so with respect to their power base.

It is the personal responsibility of leaders to push themselves to their furthest abilities, constantly bettering themselves, the hierarchy, and those below them that form the body of the structure. To be a leader at the head of the pyramid is not to pull all of the vigor out of the body, slowly killing it for your own greed. To be a leader is to guide and nurture the body so as to develop growth while maintaining structural stability.

Although a leader is given the power to function from those below them, popular opinion, as in democratic systems, should not always direct the actions of the leader. The leader's job is to be a guide, a teacher, and a healer. We have all witnessed illogical mob mentality, so we can understand that popular opinion based on biased emotional fears cannot be allowed to rule the doctrine of an organization. A poor leader sways to ignorant popular opinions in order to stay in power or worse yet, encourages them as to divide the people below him into more easily manageable pieces. If the body of the pyramid sees enemies within itself, it will ignore the head. Divide and conquer; necessary for war but an absolute evil when applied to the controlling of those one is supposed to be leading.

As leaders we should focus our energies on the stability of the group; towards the educating and guiding of our followers to stabilize and better themselves, rather than forcing rigid controls upon them from the top down. In this we will also fulfill our role as healers, as in order to effectively guide and educate we must heal the divisions between our followers. The divisions of humans based on ignorance, illogic, and base emotion must be healed if we are to act, not as extreme individualists or dependents of the system, but as responsible interdependent members of a group.

Leadership positions demand capable people. Those of us who are natural leaders innately understand that we are more capable than others to lead, but we can take this the wrong way as to mean that we are better people. When leaders put themselves upon a pedestal, it severs their ties to their followers and creates not only animosity but mismanagement. If we as leaders assume that we can manage an organization single- handedly, our micromanaging will destroy the faith of our workers, fellow citizens, etc: in each other as well as their respect of the power structure itself.

Leaders must therefore realize and understand the capabilities of the people beneath them and utilize the skill sets of their followers to the fullest degree whether in production, management, or what have you. When this is done and men are not only allowed but encouraged to project their skills, faith is built between followers and leaders both.

Many in the position to lead find themselves with underlings they feel are not as capable to do their duty as the leader themselves would be in their place. We should be careful not to jump in and try to take over the duty of an unable follower. Though we may feel that the duty of our followers is better done by ourselves, when we jump in and take over or micromanage, this serves to drives a wedge that destroys faith in the group. Instead what should be done in this case is to use our position as leader to educate on how to do a duty better, encourage and guide our followers in the desired direction, and then work to heal any toes that have been stepped on.

Let us consider the following example. You are an office manager at a company that specializes in the construction of personal use black holes. You have noticed that one of your call center operators has been upsetting customers, coming in late, and has been missing his sales quota. As this person works the same hours as you do in a day, it would be impossible to really do your job as manager if you were to try and do theirs as well, wouldn't it? On top of this if you were to find a way to do both, as in standing over their shoulders and micromanaging them, then you would not only be undercutting the employee but also unwittingly encouraging his fellow workers to avoid contact with you: stripping away their faith in you as a leader, as well as breeding a sense of contempt, fear, and irritability in them for their personal space being invaded.

What we may do instead that will serve to better group cohesion, productivity and individual mindset is this: Instead of jumping the gun and assuming our worker cannot do the job, we should talk to them and find out what the personal issue is. Are they bored, is there a problem at home, were they not trained well enough? Let's presume they are bored. Rather than chastise someone for being bored and not toeing the line, perhaps they need to move on to another job, transfer to a different section within the company, or maybe they just find their work dull because they have the mental ability to do much more. Before we can guide and direct others we must first educate ourselves. This done, we can guide them into a position that better suits them, or reorganize their current duties to give them more individual freedom to create productive results. We can also educate them about the company structure and career paths within it as to help them not only set goals for future development of the company and individual, but also so that the worker may have hope, something to look forward to on the dull days or weeks that are unavoidable.

After all this we come to healing. We have caught the problem, addressed and implemented a solution, but as in any disagreement their can still be negative emotions left behind. It is important then that we address any of these emotions in the worker, or they may fester and grow into future problems. Did they feel talked down to? Did they feel stupid? Were they embarrassed? Do they have a problem with the way in which the issue was approached? In order for the group to heal, function, and grow, the individuals that construct it must also do the same. Following the healing of the person, the rift they have caused within the company will heal, and with that stability and functionality is found.

A leader must be selfless. The aggrandizement of self, built from the toil of our followers is a sad offense. If a group is led honorably and successfully, without selfishness on the part of the leader, then the members of this group will reward the leader and the organization in the form of productivity, efficiency, positive attitude and stability. We must not set out from the start with the idea of self before all others. Others before Self in matters public; Self before others in matters private. This is to say, when we interact with others it is necessary that we should attempt to hold their interests as our primary concerns and not push our views upon them but rather seek to find common ground in a social sense. When we are in contemplation or in private spaces, we should not concern ourselves with the views of others so much as we are rather more concerned with understanding ourselves and fulfilling our own desires. As leaders we must learn to balance the needs of the self, the group, and other individuals.

We must as leaders understand that long term stability is of higher value than short term gain. We must not make sacrifices of those under our control unless warranted for the long-term stability of the group, not for the short-term profit of a few. As leaders, we must be comfortable in the delegation of organizational responsibilities to our followers, and understand the fact that we are dealing with people suffering from the human condition, not robots that can recreate in an instant what it is that the we ourselves would or could do in their shoes. As leaders we must be personally responsible, selfless, dignified, honorable, respectful, understanding, educating, guiding, healing, thoughtful, curious, socially aware, adaptive, creative, and excessively loyal to our fellow human beings.

Discipline

Images of storm troopers, reclusive monks, martial arts masters and self-made billionaire industrialists fill our imaginations when we think of discipline. We think of the success of a soldier as being driven by their self-sacrifice through discipline, the years lost to training by the monk, the businessman and martial artist for the same reasons. Discipline though is not something that is only possessed by those at the extreme.

Discipline is key to all of us who do not wish to wait forever upon chance. "God helps those who help themselves" they say. Though discipline over ourselves is necessary to achieve a small amount of material freedom, it is important for us to remember that, although we sacrifice contentment of the Self (our full openness in the now) so that we may more fully enjoy our future, we must not forget to care for our Self, our state of mind, and our state of spiritual well-being.

As we spoke of before, material wealth cannot bring happiness in and of itself. If we spend all of our time chasing a dream, we will leave our Self behind. This is much like the rich man that works all his life to attain riches, then when reaching middle age and achieving all of his monetary goals, he suddenly breaks down as he looks around at all of his life filled with empty things and surrounded by empty friends. He realizes that all of his discipline and self-sacrifice have been all for naught, for he has no Self to identify, only himself as defined by the material possessions he has. He does not know who he is.

We are defined by our actions. It is what we do in a day to day, minute to minute world that makes us who we are. If we waste all of our discipline in the wrong area, if we direct all of our actions poorly, we are nothing but hard-driving and emotionless machines of our own design, knocking down everything in the way of our goals with no worries for what beauty or chance intrigue we destroy along the way.

      A disciplined mind should not be relegated only to worldly matters as we find in many cases, but spiritual and mental health should be equally disciplined. Man is made of three parts: spirit, mind, and body. It is the interactions of these three divisions that make life what it is for us, and it is the willful balancing of these that produces a harmonious and contented existence. This willful balancing of our own trinity is the most important form of self-discipline. All lower forms of self-discipline are mastered when this balance is in stasis, as all aspects of ourselves falls within this trinity of Self. We must discipline our minds. We must discipline our spirits. We must discipline our bodies. Achieve balance. Realize Enlightenment.

37.

Crime

    We determine our definitions of crime based upon our socialized values and specifically on our own personal values. Crime, like everything else in this world, is not easily defined within strict black and white terminology, but is heavily shaded with gray areas. What truly is crime, or criminal? Criminal behavior in one section of society may be harshly punished while similar behavior is rewarded in another. If it is acceptable for a pharmaceutical company to invest in putting people on prescriptions that they become dependent on for the sake of profit, why is it that we consider the coke dealer criminal who is simply trying to make a living?

    We bombard ourselves with countless excuses as to why this can happen and that cannot; trying to convince ourselves that our own hypocrisy is somehow warranted. "Well," we say, "Corporate drug companies are respected by the government and medical community and there must be good reason." This assumes two things: first that the government and medical community are independent of the influence of drug companies and that they not only have an unbiased opinions, but that their approval of drug companies through medical practices and government legislation is focused on the good of the people rather than for the sake of the personal profit of a few. Secondly, this assumes that we as ordinary people are not educated or mentally capable enough to form our own judgments on these issues, and so we convince ourselves that we are not really surrounded by hypocrisy but that it is just that we do not understand; and so we give up our power to the government, or powerful organizations in order that we may avoid responsibility.

In fact, the actions of countless thousands of officially approved industries across the world are as morally criminal as a street thug, and in many cases more so. There is a difference though between true crime and recognized crime. True crime is morally irresponsible action, whereas recognized crime is action which is officially recognized by an authority as criminal. Therefore, two criminals committing nearly the same crime can be given two entirely different treatments depending only upon their status within official authority's ranks.

Corruption is an unavoidable force in any society. In a civilization based upon laws such as our own, where we celebrate the industriousness and power of the individual over group well-being, it is inevitable that we should have laws that protect industry and power-hungry people at the expense of the we the people. It is also forseen that the standards expected to be followed by those being ruled are not to be expected of those who do the ruling; for those in power perpetuate their reign through the funding of legislators and government officials, influencing through independent think tanks, media campaigns, and even public education. This multi-tiered influence over social institutions allows the values of those in power to be official recognized and enforced by the state regardless of their morality or hypocrisy. When common sense is outlawed as politically incorrect, there is an obvious problem.

It is quite irresponsible for us to pawn off our opinions of criminality upon others as it leads to further criminality. It is the laziness of mind that leads to corruption in the first place, while the same laziness allows corruption to perpetuate itself. A lack of personal responsibility starting with one man spreads like a virus infecting others until an entire society is full of self-serving criminals. This is after all what corruption in society is: morally criminal irresponsibility and selfishness at the expense of others.

We cannot truly speak of crime unless we speak of where our view of crime comes from. If our socialized values identifying criminality are based upon illogical arguments and grand hypocrisies, it is quite clear that we ought to question and resolve our beliefs. As painful as it may be to go against our own socialization it is imperative to the health of mankind that we constantly strive to better humanity and civilization through the betterment of ourselves. Betterment and growth cannot be achieved when all we are doing is repeating the same errors over and over again simply because they are comfortable for us.

When we allow ourselves to make the same mistakes over and over again, we are allowing our institutions to make repetitive mistakes as well, and hence we allow true criminals to go free and force false criminals to be persecuted under immoral recognized law. All this, for the sake of sloth.

38.

Personal Responsibility

So much of what holds humanity together stems from personal responsibility. Ranging from family to clan and from city to nation, stability is dependent upon the personal responsibilities of those individuals that together form the group. When we become lax in taking responsibility for our own action, society falls apart. On a more localized level, relationships crumble.

In a society such as ours, where those before us have built up such an economic fortress that enables nearly all of us to not only have our basic needs addressed, but for the general population to live at relative ease in comparison to other nations around the world, we have the tendency to become lax in our responsibilities. This tendency surfaces as a result of such abundance being more easily obtained by each successive generation. We who grow up knowing nothing else can feel that this constant abundance and ease of life is owed to us.

To make the assumption that our way of life is ordinary when we have experienced no deviation from this assumption is not surprising; in fact it is our natural tendency to adapt in such a fashion. Though this is an understandable assumption, it is far from being an acceptable one. We must as free-thinking individuals constantly question what is the status quo; not only on the outside but on the inside. It is generally the smallest and most subtle assumptions that direct our world views. How do we spot something as standing out when it permeates almost everything we encounter? Such a thing as self-responsibility or lack thereof is constantly addressed in social undertones.

If we are given everything without putting in any work from childhood well into adulthood, it should go without saying that without proper guidance we will likely live the rest of our lives expecting to be given whatever we desire regardless of our own actions. Millions of people today live in such a fashion with the popularization and widespread use of welfare programs throughout the modernized world.

These programs are set up to help clothe, shelter, and feed people; but though their ideals are honorable, the administration of these programs serves to further erode society and perpetuates the problem. There is an old saying everyone has heard that states "Give a man a fish and he'll eat for a day, teach a man to fish and he'll feed himself for a life time". These programs teach people not how to fend for themselves but rather how to remain dependent upon a system of support. Even worse, once people are dependent upon such a system and feel that what they are given is owed them, they will then seek to corrupt and exploit the system further for their own personal gain and in effect take away the care from others who rightfully need it.

This is just one example of social reinforcement that encourages us to shed our own personal responsibility. In this example alone we can see the seeds and fruits of corruption, exploitation, self-interest over group interests, lack of personal responsibility, and well-meaning but ill-administered ideals. Now compile a list in your mind of all the other similar social reinforcements and multiply the negative effects exponentially off into the distance!

Spoiled rich kids that never work for anything even after adulthood, poor kids that live off welfare into adulthood, middle class kids that never do hard work because they think it is below them, and seek the simplest job with the least responsibility for the most money in adulthood: All of these children, millions of them, grow up in a society that rewards the shedding of personal responsibility. All of them will grow up and raise their own children the same way. What happens then after only two or three generations of general disregard for personal responsibility, with a positive reinforcement placed instead upon selfish and inconsiderate behavior?

      The breakdown of the common sense that maintains a society is directly correlated to the uprising of self-serving behavior in that society. Therefore although personnel in a bank may understand what they are doing is damaging the stability of the society from which they make their profit, they remain unconcerned because they are more concerned with personal profit than with systematic stability. Why be responsible when it means that we will not be able to buy a new house or a new car? When throwing others under the bus for profit becomes a standard practice, what choice do we have when we are in competition with others that embrace such morals?

      If individual mindsets and systems that destroy personal responsibility are not immediately disposed of, they continuously infect others with their ideals until the only way to fight these forces is to become just as corrupt as they are, or leave. Those who do take responsibility for their actions, who are forced to stay in such an environment at some point must cave and become corrupted themselves in order to survive. From here our children become corrupted and are likely to become even more so than us, for what is done once to the parent in their lifetime is made acceptable to our children and therefore will be done unto them far more often.

For example let us say that Medicare legislation is passed in the time of your father that socializes medical care for people that are incapable of funding their own care. This precedent set, it is then more likely for you to accept legislation that gives further power and money to this program: perhaps giving money to single mothers with jobs that only pay this or that amount, or similar situations where funding it not so much determined by incapability as it is determined by the drive of a person to provide for themselves. The corruption of legislation grows larger from one generation to the next, until a society is ruled not by principles of common sense and personal responsibility but by laws reinforcing selfishness and inconsideration.

It is what it is. It would be nice if personal responsibility were held on a pedestal and greed was ground into the dirt, but that is not the way of large populations with centralized governments. In order for the centralized government to work it must make the people dependent upon it, lest they may want to rule themselves.

What we must strive to do as free and responsible people is to reinforce our belief through action. We must not follow through on half measures such as social programs that only mask symptoms while allowing the sickness to grow. Rather then feeding others, we should be providing them the means of feeding themselves. Rather than seeking to consolidate our own wealth and giving scraps to others, we ought to be working to ensure the well-being of others as often as we do ourselves, and consider the stability of the family, city, and state not as something separate and second in importance to our own well being, but as something primary and necessary to it.

Personal responsibility must be taught to children and then reinforced when they are adults. In order to do this we as parents must take the responsibility upon ourselves to teach our children values and not defer such teaching to schools or other social programs. Self-reliance must then be imposed upon the education systems as an ideal they must reinforce and uphold in their students. These students will take this viewpoint out into the world with them and be a counter to the culture of selfish non-responsibility. As adults influencing their society, our children can tear down negative social bulwarks and build in their place others that are of positive influence to current and upcoming generations.

To do good on a massive scale takes massive cooperation of good people, while to do evil and corrupt only takes one person acting while good people stand aside and do nothing. Good people hold themselves responsible for their lives and the lives of those around them. We must take actions to defend and propagate the best of humanity. Otherwise, we really aren't good people, are we?

Personal responsibility is the foundation of individuals and societies alike. Without this concept being realized, we wander about life as zombies pulled along by false conceptions in a doubly illusory existence. Societies crumble as their citizens consume the straws that make up the house that is civilization, fueling the fires of corrupted desires.

Girls & Boys

I remember being very young and asking my father about women and him responding with a shrug, a smirk, and thoughtful eyes. He said, "If you ever figure them out, make sure and tell me." We can talk all day about existentialism or the nuances of regional trade agreements; we can ramble on about our hobbies, jobs and houses. At the end of the day we almost always end up concerned not about these things, but rather
with the opposite sex. To some it seems absurd that we should have so much art, science, industry, trade, hoards of high-minded human creations surrounding us, and yet still be so wrapped up in our baseness, devoted to capturing and holding the love of another.

Truly though, absurdity is only attached our base natures when we believe that human nature and human mind are separable from each other. Most of us live in a comfortable balance of mind and body, finding nothing whatsoever audacious about seeking a mate and the constant battle to retain and gain their affections. For us the absurdity in love is not in its theosophical attributes, but rather in the opposite sex's ability to completely confound us and leave our thoughts scrambled, our emotions running wild, and our bodies ill.

We are gluttons for pain in the arena of love and so we soldier on undaunted, hoping the next time we will either figure out what is going on with the opposite sex or that the love sickness we find in failure will just finish us off for good. Love sickness and heartbreak are inevitable to us, as our youth, stupidity, and stubbornness play large parts in our failures. These failures though are important in our education of the sexes. After a time we begin to figure out what we can do and what we cannot, as well as what we should and should not. Year after year, decade after decade, we interact with and educate ourselves upon the sexes, yet there is for many of us an undetected or misunderstood variable that we just cannot put our collective finger on.

The chief cause of our confusion and frustration is not that we are not trying, and not that we are idiots, but that the opposite sex has an opposing mindset to our own. It is in our assumption that we ALL think alike that causes great frustration among many of us. Naturally our similar assumptions when dealing with the opposite sex cause equally formidable frustrations.

Often times we go so far as to describe the opposite sex as a separate species. We innately understand that there is a vast chasm in world view between men and women but it seems so overwhelmingly large that we cannot bring ourselves to comprehend the minds of our other halves. It all really boils down to our own personal comfort zones. The more likely we are to be comfortable in our own skin, the better able we are to relate to others in general. The more open we are to relating with others in general, the better able we are to open our minds to understand the mindsets of the opposite sex.

If we are able to view the world without prejudging it, if we hold a fluid mindset rather than one that is fixed and obscured by denials, then we are able to try on another person's head as a talented actor does. To really understand the opposite sex as fully as we can, we must be comfortable in not only our own skins but in the heads of other people. We must not be threatened that through learning we may lose ourselves, but rather we must be confident that through new experience we will come into better understanding of ourselves. If we are able to turn off our defensiveness and judgment of others, we can begin to grasp the basic differences in mind between the male and female.

    The nature of men is to be content. If it weren't for the nurturing and driving efforts of women we would most likely still be living in caves and throwing our poop at passers-by. Granted as disgusting as females may find the idea, most men raised in such conditions would likely remain content and as happy as a clam living day to day at the whims of nature. Men see the world in general as it is; more so than as it was or as it should be. Men are the ones that keep the bumper sticker printers of "carpe diem" and "no fear" in business. Because men think more of where they are than where they should be or where they could go, they are more likely to see risk not as danger but as something fun, a challenge.

    As a boy I saw that I could jump out of a tree at ten feet and land the fall with no injury, so why not try higher? Eventually I worked my way up to a homemade zip line from sixty feet, finding myself holding onto a busted up old ten-speed bicycle handle for dear life. I almost met my end on this adventure when I bounced on the line, lost grip of the handle (which went sailing into the air like a pebble from a slingshot), and fell thirty or forty feet. The scream of terror I had been trying with all my power to push out of my lungs, but was incapable of doing, suddenly was exhaled in a large whoosh as my breath was knocked out by an inconsiderate patch of earth rushing at me, as if it couldn't take just one break from the laws of physics. As I lay on the ground wondering if I was ever going to be able to coerce my lungs to breath again, my hearing began turning sound back into recognizable forms, just in time for me to realize the panic in the voices of my brother and his friends. Wondering what the fuss was all about and not being able to even crawl, I used all my strength to roll in their general direction. In an imperceptible instant after my one roll, the ten-speed handles buried themselves halfway deep in the pile of dirt precisely where, a moment before, the torso carrying my useless lungs had been. This for boys is fun. I'll never understand what is so fascinating about playing house with a stuffed zebra and drinking empty glasses of imaginary tea.

For men there is an innate (although often unconscious) understanding that time is short. The communication of men therefore reflects this in its abruptness. The dialogue of men is filled with abbreviations, short words, and short sentences, and is most often straight and to the point. Our personal experiences and scientific studies show us that men use far less words per day than women to express themselves. It is the difference in our use of language to express ourselves that causes the main miscommunications between the sexes.

As is their nature, men speak straightforwardly about their thoughts whereas women speak a more subtle language based in subtext. It is in our assumption of the opposite sexes' ability to speak our own language that causes misunderstanding, and hence arguments, anger, sadness, and confusion arise. Men assume that when women speak they are speaking outrightly and that they mean directly what they say, while women assume that men understand the subtext and subtle connotations of the female language.

Women are the nurturers and inspirations of society. It is for women that men have built the world's museums that are the homes to paintings and sculptures from across time, depicting the beauty of the female form and the grace of the mother. The statement, "Behind every great man, resides a greater woman," reveals the importance of women in the shaping of the world. Woman's nature, unlike man's tendency towards contentedness with his situation in the world, is to improve upon the world in a relentless fashion. Biologically women are constructed in order that they may best nurture and protect for the family, whereas men are constructed that they may better provide for and defend the family. Where men historically have provided labor for the family, women have directed the labor of men, sometimes directly and sometimes indirectly. As woman's tendency is towards protection of the family, the duties of nesting, nurturing, teaching, etc., fall to her in that by controlling these duties she is indeed ensuring the future protection of the family.

    Typical problems arise when men and women find themselves in disagreement over the smallest of issues. A man may go and make a small purchase such as alcohol for the weekend with his friends. He may view this as a harmless act whereas the woman that he is involved with may see this as an act of war. It may be that she has recently had a conversation with him in which she felt her point had gotten across about saving money for a purchase for the family. If though she attempted to allude to her wishes through feminine subtext rather than in masculine straightforward wording, it is most likely that he had no idea what she was talking about, and will have no idea what it is he is going to be in trouble for when he gets home.

    The two very separate natures of men and women lead to constant bitterness so long as the two parties do not agree to disagree. Relations with the opposite sex revolve around the needs of the two people involved. When one party decides to seize control of the relationship, rather than simply sharing their half of responsibilities, the relationship ceases to do any sort of relating whatsoever and instead becomes a power struggle of "I'm right, you're wrong."

The entire point of creating an interpersonal relationship with a member of the opposite sex is so that we may form a loving bond that allows us to feel more ourselves than when we are by ourselves, not so that one may try and force upon the other their own will. If we either outrightly or deceitfully seek to control those whom we purport to love, do we really love them or just an idealized version of them that lives in our mind?

For the sake of mutual happiness and a functional relationship: Guys, be honest, ask questions when you don't understand, and don't expect your life to go unchanged by a woman. Ask the women in your lives to understand that you say what you mean and you don't have any ulterior motives. Ladies, be patient with the men in your lives, and explain to them in plain speech when they don't understand your subtext, and don't expect him to change into someone else. Teach them to differentiate between what you say and what you mean. We must respect our differences just as we do our similarities. All of us need to bare our thoughts and feelings openly, agree to disagree, and learn to share the reigns of power over our shared lives.

Body & Mind

Like everything else in life, we need to learn to balance our bodies and our minds. Many of us read, and write, and think all day, but can not even walk more than a few steps without being winded. Many of us also do nothing but play sports, games, and work out. For the sake of a healthy life experience it is of great importance that we are healthy in all aspects mental, physical and spiritual.

When we begin to allow our systems to get out of balance our abilities fall into atrophy. Just as our muscles shrink and turn to fat when we stop exercising them, our minds are unable to calculate properly when unused.

There is an effect that balancing physical exercise and mental exercise has which often goes unnoticed. One may assume that working out has nothing to do with their mental capabilities because they are already extremely intelligent, but it is important for us to realize that physical exercise can effect not just the rapidity and accuracy of thought, but our outlook on life.

All thoughts that we have, and all actions that are followed by them, are affected by our positive or negative world-views. When we exercise regularly and our bodies are producing the natural chemicals that humans experience in the wild, we feel much more ourselves. This feeling breeds a sense of power over one's life and brings about a positive outlook.

When we have a positive outlook, a healthy body, and a healthy mind, our thoughts in day to day life take the form of action, and our thoughts then become realized in the material world in a positive fashion. There are many ways to be lethargic and slothful, and they all affect us in negative fashions.

Death

What do any of us know about death? What are we so afraid of? We are afraid of leaving this plane of existence and this body, the only thing we have ever known. We are afraid of the end, blackness.

There is no death to be afraid of; we do not exist separate of God. This separate life and body, as readily illustrated prior to this chapter, is only a temporary illusion. The reason we are having this illusion in the end boils down to self-imposed isolation. Much like the monk will isolate himself for his betterment, our true Self is isolating itself within this body for the sake of purification.

The "I" that we consider ourselves is only our ego. When we successfully strip away our layers of self-deceptions and make our inner Self clear to view, we find that there is nothing at all impermanent about the Self. Some call it a soul, or a spirit, again it doesn't matter what it is called. What matters is that IT is there, and is in all of us. It is awareness, a consciousness, and it is inherent in existence.

This infinite awareness is the ground of existence and can never die. Matter/energy may change forms or cross dimensions, but doesn't just come to an end, it transforms. Likewise we, awareness incarnate (incarcerated), transform when this body dies. To paraphrase a little green wise man, "We are not creatures of this crude matter, we are beings of light." This light is the Holy Spirit, and WE are infinite.

42.

Quality of Life

The quality of our lives is dependent upon the individual self, not upon external conditions. Though the illusion of self is formed partly from external sources, it is not fully dependent upon them for its continued existence. Our happiness and contentedness, as well as our unhappiness, is conditioned by the way in which the Self allows external inputs to affect it. Some by their nature will never be able to help themselves nor ever be able to be helped by others. For many of us though, whether through genetics and conditioning, by way of spiritual incarnation, or both, possess the ability within ourselves to govern the Self and guide our state of awareness.

For those of us blessed in this manner, we are able to ensure our quality of life regardless of the environment in which we are placed. Thanks to the Beatles we know that "Money can't buy me love." We understand that our will controls our experience and our mindset, so we are not dependent upon "things" and "stuff" or particular "conditions" to make us happy; rather we are contented in our sustained awareness. We allow ourselves to be contented simply by the experience of life, reveling in the senses, the mind, and in spirit. We the contented are unattached to the past or the future, only concerned with maintaining mindfulness of, and in, the ever present moment, the time of no time. We know that we will not be more happy in the future than we have allowed ourselves to be in the past, meaning NOW. We know that we must strive to be content right now, right here, always.

When we embrace our dharma, our duty, we embrace our true natures and this sets us free from karma, our past sins. For when we understand our Self in its full sense and depth, its relation to everything from the ground of all being to the smallest subatomic particle, we understand the action of no action and therefore we break free. In escaping the grasps of karma we can escape samsara, our own personal hell on earth; for we see that all that makes us suffer is only a preference within ourselves. When we realize experientially that Heaven is inseparable from Hell we are truly free.

If you are one of those able to, as Jim Morrison put it, "break on through to the other side," to control the quality of this waking dream we call life, to live in contentedness, what are you waiting for? The only moment is now.

One must learn, that they may forget.

Cameron Smietana is an incorrigible scamp.

Before writing this book he was born, grew up, fell out of a few trees, drove too fast, had a few brushes with death, went to college, had his heart broken and broke a few hearts, ran out of money, racked up debt, worked as a delivery boy, got married, joined the military, got divorced, worked at a record store, paid off some financial and karmic debts, traveled the world, smoked a lot of cigarettes, drank a lot of whiskey, and worked as a defense contractor in the Middle East.

www.ingramcontent.com/pod-product-compliance
Lightning Source LLC
Chambersburg PA
CBHW061644040426
42446CB00010B/1570